KORN/FERRY INTERNATIONAL
powered by LOMINGER

Becoming an

Agile
Leader

*A Guide to Learning
From Your Experiences*

J. Evelyn Orr

Becoming an Agile Leader

A Guide to Learning From Your Experiences

Tel. +1 952-345-3610
Tel. +1 877-345-3610 (US / Canada)
Fax. +1 952-345-3601
www.kornferry.com
www.lominger.com

ISBN 978-1-933578-39-2

Item number 82161

1st Printing April 2012

To Maya, Albert, Nelson, Muhammad, Mary Kay,
and other leaders past and present
who inspire others
with a sense of purpose and possibility.

To John, Solveig, and Soren
who inspire me every day.

Table of Contents

Introduction: Becoming Learning Agile

Imagine a biographer took you on as a project. The goal would be to uncover key events in your life and illustrate how these key events influenced your personality, career choice, leadership style, and accomplishments.

If your biographer asked you to name the key experiences in your life that shaped who you are and how you lead, how would you respond? Why did those experiences have a lasting impact on you? How did you approach them? What did you learn as a result?

It has often been said that we are the sum total of our experiences. This book proposes that we are the sum total of what we *learn* from our experiences.

While we enter the world with some qualities embedded in our genetic code, the power of experiences should not be underestimated. In his book *True North*, Bill George interviewed 125 exceptional leaders and could not find a single common skill or attribute that explained their success. The one common factor that did emerge was that they all sought out and were changed by life experiences. "By constantly testing themselves through real-world experiences and by reframing their life stories to understand who they are, these leaders unleashed their passions and discovered the purpose of their leadership."[1]

The question becomes how to harness the power of experiences. Your plans may include climbing the corporate ladder, starting a community group, holding a political office, or providing innovative thinking on tough problems. No matter what form your leadership takes, you are operating in an increasingly complex world which requires you to be resourceful, adaptive, and have a learner's mind-set. Learning from your experiences becomes a critical tool for success under these demanding conditions.

Leaders who have the greatest impact and the best results have more experiences and learn more from those experiences than average leaders.[2,3] This is true for leaders around the world.[4,5,6,7] When asked to describe what they took away from an experience, the most effective leaders relay numerous, nuanced lessons, while average leaders note fewer, more superficial lessons.[2,3] It is no surprise, then, that when faced with new challenges, leaders who have wrested more meaning from their past experiences will have more guiding principles to draw upon. This ability to glean numerous, rich, memorable lessons from experiences and apply them effectively in future situations is known as Learning Agility.[8]

Exceptional leadership stands at the intersection of the right experiences and the ability to learn from those experiences.

Fortunately, neither Learning Agility nor our experiences are fixed. Experiences can be sought out. Knowing which experiences have the most developmental potential can equip you with the ability to develop the skills that will get you where you want to go. Learning Agility is something that can be developed. Changing and growing as a result of experiences can be accomplished through focused, conscious reflection and making the effort to incorporate lessons in new situations.

This book illustrates how to seek out and learn from experiences that will enrich your life, build your leadership skills, and make you more effective in what you do.

Finding the Right Experiences

It's important to recognize that not all experiences are created equal. Some experiences are more developmental than others. You learn more when an experience is challenging for you. Challenging experiences are those that are new, different, or have high stakes. But take care that it is the right amount of challenge. A challenge that is too far beyond your capacity or skills may only serve to deter you from seeking out other challenging experiences.

How will you know if an experience is challenging enough to spark some learning? If the experience meets most of the following criteria, it will likely be an experience you can learn from:[9]

Success is not guaranteed

Responsibility rests with you

Requires working with new people or a lot of people

Stakes and pressure are high

Requires influencing without authority

Different from what you've done before

Your work will be under scrutiny

New territory for the organization or community

Requires you to be resourceful

Tests your ability to deal with complexity and ambiguity

Involves some hurdles

When an experience takes you out of your comfort zone, pushes you beyond your normal routine and habits, and your usual approach or modus operandi does not apply, then you know that it is a developmental, challenging assignment. The best learning experiences are emotional, require you to take risks, and tend to have real-life consequences. Hesitation, mild dread, trepidation, and resistance are all signs that you are encountering an experience that will stretch you. Going against your natural grain is not a comfortable feeling, but it is a prerequisite for personal growth.[10]

Finding the right experiences depends on your life goals, career ambitions, and skill gaps. What do you aspire to? Do you see yourself becoming an executive leader for a multinational corporation someday? Or are you aiming to be instrumental in bringing about social or political change at a local, national, or global level? No matter which direction you choose, you will need to seek experiences that will prepare you for the demands of that particular role.

Whatever your destination or ambition, conventional wisdom (based in science) prevails: we learn best by doing. There is no substitute for real-world, on-the-job experiences to prepare you for greater challenges. These are experiences you can actively pursue—seize the opportunity to study or work abroad, find a job in a different department, form a new team, or take on a difficult project where predecessors failed to make headway.

For over three decades, researchers have studied how successful leaders learn from experience. In multiple studies, over 350 successful leaders around the world shared the key experiences and lessons learned from those experiences that made a lasting impact on their leadership. In study after study, the same types of experiences emerged as being the most impactful and developmental experiences for leaders.[2,5,6,7]

The Most Developmental Experiences[11]

Leading or contributing to a project or task force

Managing a change

Managing a crisis

Making a cross-move

Fixing or turning around something

Formulating strategic plans

Taking an international assignment

Moving from a business line to a support function (or vice versa)

Increasing the size and scale of your job

Increasing the scope and complexity of your job

Managing people and dealing with people issues

Influencing without authority

Initiating a start-up (a new team, product line, or process)

Being an entrepreneur

Aside from experiences you seek out, another type of experience is one that is uninvited: hardship. Hardships come in the form of bad luck, bad circumstances, or bad decisions. Getting fired, having a nightmare boss, getting a divorce, struggling with personal health issues, and facing discrimination are examples of the kinds of adversity that not only test one's resilience but instigate deeper introspection. Hardships provide an opportunity to look inward, to recognize personal limitations, reevaluate priorities, and make personal changes.[2]

Regardless of the type of experience, people who are more learning agile are able to extract more valuable lessons from the same challenging experiences.

Becoming Learning Agile

Learning Agility is formally defined as *the willingness and ability to learn from experience, and subsequently apply that learning to perform successfully under new or first-time conditions.* Another way of looking at it is that learning agile people *know what to do when they don't know what to do.*[12]

People who are learning agile are not only better equipped to get the most out of challenging experiences, they are more willing to seek out new and different experiences. In fact, the lessons they take away from their experiences often build self-awareness, cognitive flexibility, relationship management, adaptability, and resourcefulness—all behaviors associated with Learning Agility. So it becomes a self-reinforcing cycle. Not only does learning from your experiences help develop your Learning Agility—Learning Agility helps you learn more from your experiences.[12]

Learning agile leaders seek out novel, varied, and challenging experiences; they learn more from those experiences; and they are drawn to new challenges. Because of their diverse experiences and the amount of time they spend making sense of those experiences, learning agile leaders develop more skills and perform better in new and challenging jobs.[2,3,13]

Greater
Learning
Agility

Even More
Challenging
Experiences

Learning
Agility

New
Experiences

Experiences

Lessons

Richer
Lessons

The qualities of learning agile people take shape in five particular ways...[14, 15]

Self-Awareness

They know what they're good at
and not so good at and actively
address the not so good

Mental Agility

They are critical thinkers who are comfortable
with complexity, examine problems carefully,
and make fresh connections that they make
understandable to others

People Agility

They understand the value of getting
things done through others and are
exceptional communicators who see conflict
as an opportunity rather than a problem

Change Agility

They like to experiment and can deal
with the discomfort of change; they
have a passion for ideas and are highly
interested in continuous improvement

Results Agility

They deliver results in first-time
situations through resourcefulness
and having a significant presence
that inspires others

Not all learning agile people excel in all five areas. And Learning Agility is not like an on/off switch where people either have it or they don't. Most people possess a moderate degree of Learning Agility and a few people are highly learning agile.[10]

People who are more learning agile tend to be curious and are willing to take risks and make mistakes. They are keen observers of themselves, others, and situations—constantly inquiring about the dynamics of the situation and making sense of it. The highly learning agile have more ideas for how to learn, more approaches to solving a problem, more tactics at hand. By making comparisons and drawing parallels, they see trends and patterns that others may miss. Making sense of everything they reflect on, they distill their insights into guiding principles that they can apply in future situations.

Underlying the entire process is a mindfulness or a consciousness that maximizes learning. To the extent that this mindful reflection and application can be learned and repeated, everyone who wishes can further develop their Learning Agility.

Learning from Your Experiences

Finding an approach that helps you extract the richest lessons from any experience will help you develop your skills and Learning Agility. While you shouldn't underestimate how difficult it is to harvest and incorporate lessons learned, it is possible to improve upon.

> It's one thing to make a list of lessons, quite another to master them. These lessons are not delivered with spellbinding clarity; they must be dug out of complex, confusing, ambiguous situations. Even when they are delivered up, they are tough to incorporate. Especially for executives, learning is a murky business, occurring in fits and starts over time. Lessons accumulate, evolve, affect one another, gain potency in combination, don't take the first time, atrophy, and get forgotten. Some are much tougher to learn than others, and the toughest part of all may be using what one has learned to make a difference on the job.
>
> (From *The Lessons of Experience: How Successful Executives Develop on the Job.* (1988). M. W. McCall Jr., M. M. Lombardo, and A. M. Morrison. New York, NY: The Free Press. Reprinted with permission of Simon & Schuster, Inc.)

So how do you intentionally practice learning from experience? In order to make learning more deliberate and repeatable, here is a suggested process:

Experience – Seek out a challenging experience and immerse yourself in it...

What will push you beyond
what you already know how to do?

What difficult task seems undoable?

Where are there significant obstacles
that need to be overcome?

Observe – Stay mindful as you notice how the situation unfolds...

What history or background information
could be helpful?

Who are the players involved?

What is the desired outcome?

Reflect – Take the time to make sense of the experience...

Why did you choose to approach
the situation the way you did?

What felt most challenging? Why?

What did you find surprising? Why?

Distill – Extract insight, wisdom, rules of thumb, or guiding principles from the experience...

What would you do differently next time?

What meaning do you attribute to the experience?

How would you coach someone going through
a similar experience?

Apply – Find ways to use those lessons in other situations...

What lessons equip you for taking on bigger challenges?

How do the lessons you learned reframe how
you think about or approach new experiences?

What are some underlying similarities
in the new situations you encounter?

You can use this process to learn from your past, present, and future experiences. Of course, there are some obstacles to learning that might get in your way. Seeking new, different, challenging experiences where failure is a possibility is a scary prospect. Worrying about the unknown, looking stupid, losing control, or doing something wrong can all stop you before you get started. Take some time to consider what specific things might get in your way and how to deal with those obstacles before you begin. Finding ways to overcome your trepidation, summoning the courage to act in the face of fear, or constructing a mental or social safety net will be keys to opening yourself up to new learning opportunities.

How to Use This Book

This book is designed to help you learn from your experiences and build your Learning Agility. Each chapter is centered on one of the five factors of Learning Agility (Self-Awareness, Mental Agility, People Agility, Change Agility, and Results Agility) and the qualities and behaviors that exemplify each factor. After briefly exploring the qualities of Learning Agility, the focus shifts from what it is to how people develop it.

Each chapter highlights exceptional leaders who are archetypes of Learning Agility. These leaders come from a broad spectrum of fields, such as science, the arts, business, and politics. A close look at their key life experiences and lessons learned illustrates how each one became so adept at an aspect of Learning Agility. In effect, the hood is lifted on how the person came to be agile.

After gaining an understanding of other people's journeys, the focus then turns to you. Exercises and questions guide your reflection on key events in your own life—past, present, and future. You'll find these exercises at the end of each chapter and space at the back of the book for your notes.

"We had the experience but missed the meaning. And approach to the meaning restores the experience in a different form."

T. S. Eliot – Playwright, poet, and Nobel Prize winner in literature

Harvest lessons from past experiences

Take the opportunity to reflect on past experiences. The good news is that it is never too late to learn from your experiences. Take a mental trip back in time to the situation, people, and feelings that you experienced. Be curious. Ponder how you approached the situation, why you did what you did, what you took away from the experience. In asking yourself these questions, you are unleashing the power of that experience and taking valuable lessons from it that you can apply to new situations. You've had the experience. It's not too late to make sense of it.

Extract lessons from current experiences

Often, we are so immersed in present experiences that it is hard to step back and observe them as the developmental opportunities they are. Think about current projects you are on, struggles you are experiencing, changes that you are going through in your life or career. The things that cause you the most stress are probably the experiences that are ripe for reflection and learning.

Thoughtfully plan for future experiences and lessons

When you have a sense of what is important for you to develop or learn, you can proactively seek out the experiences that will help you build that skill. Knowing why you are going after a certain experience and anticipating what you want to get out of it will help guide your reflection and learning process.

Harvesting lessons from past experiences, extracting lessons from current experiences, and planning ahead for future experiences all assist you in harnessing the power of your own experiences to enhance your Learning Agility.

Learning Agility Factor

The degree to which an individual has personal insight, clearly understands their own strengths and weaknesses, is free of blind spots, and uses this knowledge to perform effectively

Self-

Awareness

Seeking Personal Insight

Self-Awareness:
Seeking Personal Insight

To be self-aware is to know yourself, to understand your strengths and limitations. It means having a tendency to seek feedback and act on it. Being introspective about mistakes and failures in order to learn from them. And staying on the lookout for new experiences to help refine or learn new skills. Internal reflection enables the expression of thoughts, feelings, and opinions with candor.

Examples

Being honest with yourself about strengths and weaknesses

Asking for feedback

Taking constructive feedback to heart and acting on it

Knowing why you're feeling a certain way

Willing to admit mistakes but not dwell on them

Looking for new personal insights

There are people who are so grounded in their sense of self, so in tune with their thoughts and feelings that they exude an authentic and unaffected demeanor. Have you noticed how you feel more at ease and relaxed in their presence? Self-aware people are not in conflict with themselves. They are in tune with their thoughts and identity. And their inner lives are reflected in their outer lives. This harmony is built and reinforced by a continual cycle of examination and insight.

"Leadership is authenticity, not style."

– Bill George

Bill George is a professor of management practice at Harvard Business School and former chairman and CEO of Medtronic. Under his leadership, Medtronic's business grew from $1.1 billion to $60 billion, an average increase of 35% per year. But George was not always a leader whom people wanted to follow. After numerous failures running for elected office in high school and at his college fraternity, he received some feedback that changed his life. A group of seniors told him point-blank that he came across as self-centered—more interested in getting ahead for personal gain than in helping other people. Though George was devastated, he took the feedback to heart and sought out more feedback from other peers. Slowly, he made changes that would shift his focus from self-interest to leadership based on communal interest.

Bill George

Jolting feedback has the potential to trigger defensiveness, but it also instigates reflection about who you are and how you are perceived. This self-examination prompts you to make changes based on where you want to be. Understanding your limits helps you draw upon other resources to achieve your objective. Knowing how and why you are feeling a certain way leads to productive channeling or resolution of those feelings. Seeing yourself as a work in progress contributes to a learning orientation so that you seek new experiences and new role models that round out something for you. Self-Awareness does not have a destination, it is not an item to check off. Building Self-Awareness is ongoing work that is never done—it becomes a habit, a practice, a journey.

Archbishop Elias Chacour, a Palestinian Christian leader and founder of the Mar Elias Educational Institutions, is someone who began practicing self-examination from an early age. As a boy, Chacour wrestled with normal childhood dilemmas like pride and jealousy. But he also encountered discrimination, animosity, and displacement from his home in a politically volatile time. He often retreated to the hills outside his village, wandering alone, talking things through, finding peace. For Chacour, reflection "proved as vital as the blood in my veins or the breath in my lungs." In his crowded boarding school, he treasured the privilege of staying up past bedtime to retreat into the pages of his journal. It was in these times of reflection that he poured out his confusion, his anger, his insecurities, his fear. By processing the source of his emotions, he could avoid acting purely from his emotions. By learning about his weaknesses, he could know when to seek support. By comparing himself to his principles, he could continue to learn and be refined. All of this inner work grounded him and prepared him for his life's work dedicated to peace and reconciliation.

Elias Chacour

Elias Chacour and Bill George are two very reflective and self-aware individuals. In fact, they have made a lifelong commitment to seeing themselves honestly so that they can be effective leaders. They balance humility in knowing their faults, mistakes, and weaknesses with confidence in knowing who they are, learning constantly, and seeking new insight. How did they come to be so grounded? So able to accept feedback and use reflection to grow personally and advance their work professionally? It may seem that some people are predisposed to seek self-reflection and a greater understanding of themselves, but it turns out that Self-Awareness is a skill that can be nurtured through the right kinds of experiences that provide fertile ground for gaining personal insights.

"You may encounter many defeats, but you must not be defeated. In fact, it may be necessary to encounter the defeats, so you can know who you are, what you can rise from, how you can still come out of it."

Maya Angelou – American poet, author, civil rights activist

Becoming Self-Aware – Maya Angelou

Let's take a deeper look at another example that highlights the learning journey toward becoming self-aware. Maya Angelou has the assuredness of a self-reflective, self-aware individual. Her ability to state the truth, her dedication to learning and improving, and her willingness to acknowledge her shortcomings with honesty and grace are qualities she learned over time from her many life experiences.

Maya Angelou is a person who has unabashedly pursued her interests and developed her sense of self. From performing calypso, gourmet cooking, acting, playwriting, making films and documentaries, writing poetry, being a single mother, learning multiple languages, and living in multiple countries, to working as a journalist, a civil rights activist, an autobiographer, and a professor, it seems that Angelou has explored every aspect of herself and the world she lives in. Along the way, she got feedback that informed her direction and her work. The feedback wasn't always flattering—ranging from rave reviews and awards to harsh criticism and rejection. Her willingness to face the truth about herself and her place in the world has enabled her to become the celebrated renaissance woman that she is today.

A look at a few of Angelou's experiences and the lessons she took from them provides us with a picture of how she developed the courage to seek out feedback, the resilience to move on from mistakes, and the hunger to gain new personal insights—all of which contributed to her remarkable wisdom and self-awareness.

Building
Self-Awareness

Maya Angelou's Experiences

1942
First Black woman streetcar conductor in San Francisco

As a 15-year-old, Maya Angelou set her mind on self-sufficiency and decided to find a job. It was San Francisco in 1942, a time and place that afforded many opportunities for working women. One job in particular caught Angelou's attention—streetcar conductorette. Her mother reminded her, "They don't accept colored people on the streetcars." But Angelou's perseverance and resourcefulness wore down the personnel director at the Market Street Railway Company, and she found herself working split shifts as the city's first Black woman streetcar conductor. Returning to school the next semester, she felt wiser because of the experience, and she had a strong sense that there was so much more to learn about herself and the world. "Without willing it, I had gone from being ignorant of being ignorant to being aware of being aware."

Small Experiences – Big Lessons

Not all lessons come from monumental or arduous events. Sometimes smaller encounters or daily realities bring a flash of insight. Many of Angelou's other experiences refined her self-awareness. Highlighted on these pages are a few experiences that contributed to her knowing herself.

Real-world experiences broaden your perspective of who you are and your place in the world

Worldly experience can be a greater teacher than the classroom

There is so much more to learn

These lessons build curiosity and the desire to seek new personal insights.

1954-1955
Ruby in *Porgy and Bess*

When Angelou joined the cast of *Porgy and Bess* in the role of Ruby, she felt extremely lucky. Over the course of a year, she toured 10 countries and 15 cities. Her many adoring fans were enchanted by her performances and would rave about her "lovely leaping legs." She received notes, flowers, and proposals for marriage. She began performing on her own at the Mars Club in Paris. The prospect of going solo and making a name for herself in Paris was tempting, but Angelou knew that she was no Josephine Baker or Billie Holiday. She remembered lessons on vanity that her grandmother imparted through stories. These lessons grounded her in humility, gratitude, and a realistic picture of who she was. This prevented her from being swept away by all the praise and compliments. Angelou realized, "I was only adequate as an entertainer, and I would never set Paris afire." Her realistic appraisal of her strengths and weaknesses influenced her decision to stay with the *Porgy and Bess* company and eventually return home to pursue other opportunities.

People can have many reasons or motives for showering praise on you

Being good enough at something will take you only so far

Vanity has the power to distort perception

These lessons encourage introspection and honest assessment of strengths and weaknesses.

Purple Onion
When working as a singer and dancer at San Francisco's Purple Onion, Angelou met Frederick Wilkerson, the vocal instructor for *Porgy and Bess*. Bluntly, he informed Angelou that her singing technique was all wrong and predicted if she continued in that manner, she would lose her voice within three years. Rather than getting defensive or discouraged, Angelou sought his counsel. Wondering how to improve, she agreed to be his student, to work hard, and listen to his feedback and coaching. Through her exposure to professional singers and vocal lessons, Angelou was fascinated to discover that the beautiful voices she heard on stage did vocal warm-ups that sounded like wounded moose, high screeches, and rusty scissors.

Preparation and training are rarely easy and never beautiful

Translation to People Agility:
Accepting criticism allows you to seek ways to improve.

Parenting advisors

As a single mother raising a son, Angelou invited many of her trusted male friends and colleagues to openly advise her on her parenting tactics. She wanted feedback on how her actions fostered or impeded her son's development. After gatherings, she would get phone calls critiquing her on her missteps. "Don't make the boy leave a game of chess—it's not about the game, it's about his manhood." "Don't tell him to get up and give his seat to a woman—give him a chance to do the right thing on his own." Angelou listened to the coaching, learned about herself as a mother, and adjusted her behavior through a few rocky but formative years in her son's upbringing. Her gratitude for these advisors is as evident as her pride in her son.

It is tempting to think you know best, but you might not

Translation to People Agility:
Asking for feedback and adjusting your personal style can improve your ability to relate to loved ones.

1958
The Harlem Writers Guild

When Angelou moved to New York City with her son, in addition to acting and performing, she began to write. She joined the Harlem Writers Guild but nearly quit after her first reading. She read her play *One Life. One Love.* Her nervousness made her hands tremble. Time slowed down as she self-consciously read the words from her pages. The room became quiet and uncomfortable. She could sense the poor reception the play was receiving. She recalls, "Even as I read, I knew the drama was bad, but maybe someone would have lied a little." The feedback was harsh. Other members were accustomed to the exchange of blunt, constructive feedback. Angelou was not. At first, she could not move from her seat. One member, John Killens, tried to convince Angelou that the unvarnished criticism was tremendously valuable and that if she appeared sensitive, she wouldn't receive such valuable feedback next time. By the end of the evening, Angelou recovered and resolved to read the group a new short story in two months' time.

Constructive feedback might be painful, but it is also valuable

Being vulnerable by sharing work with colleagues builds trust

Relying on talent is not enough; success requires hard work

These lessons build the ability to act upon constructive feedback and to learn from but not dwell on duds.

1969
First installation of
her autobiography

It took convincing, but an editor at Random House got Angelou to agree to write an autobiography. She was only 40, but already her life experiences could fill eight lives. For what became *I Know Why the Caged Bird Sings,* Angelou developed a writing ritual that she has continued to use throughout her life. She removes distractions by writing in a hotel room with no pictures on the walls and only a deck of cards, a thesaurus, a Bible, and a bottle of sherry as company. In one interview, she described that she goes through a process to enchant herself to go back in time and relive the experiences she is writing about. Her immersion in the time and place promotes reflection and helps her relay the truth about those experiences in writing.

Introspection and reflection require time, space, and concentration

Reliving an experience mentally is one way to analyze and be candid about it

These lessons promote the self-reflection required to know yourself.

Traveling the world

Traveling through Europe and Northern Africa and living in Ghana, Angelou took advantage of the opportunity to learn about local people and cultures, master five languages, and dabble in many more languages. Interacting with people all over the world afforded her the opportunity to compare and contrast her own culture, traditions, and identity. "In fact, in Ghana, I was struck by how much of what I thought was Afro-American culture really had its origin in Africa. Now I know I should have anticipated that, but I did not." These insights into her identity helped shape a documentary series on African American culture and history that she designed and wrote for PBS—*Blacks, Blues, Black!*

Seeing yourself in different contexts adds complexity and nuance to your identity

Translation to People Agility:
Knowing others helps you know yourself.

25

History, despite its wrenching pain,

Cannot be unlived, but if faced

With courage, need not be lived again.

. . . .

Lift up your hearts

Each new hour holds new chances

For a new beginning.

(From "On the Pulse of Morning" by Maya Angelou,
read by the poet at the Inauguration of
President William Jefferson Clinton on January 20, 1993)

Experiences
for building your
Self-Awareness

Angelou's Lessons Influenced
How She Approached Her Work

"Without willing it, I had gone from being ignorant of being ignorant to being aware of being aware. And the worst part of my awareness was that I didn't know what I was aware of. I knew I knew very little, but I was certain that the things I had yet to learn wouldn't be taught to me at George Washington High School."

– Maya Angelou, *I Know Why the Caged Bird Sings*

Without the guiding force of critical feedback, Angelou might have relied on talent alone rather than working to refine herself and her work. Without the ability to look at mistakes honestly, learn from them, and move on, Angelou may have been less welcoming to the next challenge that brought the possibility of failure. Without her sense of self, Angelou might not have recognized and broken through limitations. In her own words, "Each new hour holds new chances for a new beginning."

Angelou's experiences shaped how she came to know herself. She took to heart the lessons promoting self-knowledge and honest introspection. These things were instrumental in fulfilling her potential as a performer, writer, teacher, and activist.

Building Self-Awareness by Learning from Your Experiences

While Maya Angelou's life experiences are certainly unique, at their essence there are common themes. What connections can you make between Angelou's experiences and your own? What inspiration do you draw from her journey toward becoming self-aware? Between past, present, and future, you may find that you have a strong starting point for beginning or continuing your own self-awareness journey. Both on-the-job and off-the-job experiences can help you develop your courage to seek feedback, dive into your shadow side to analyze weaknesses and shortcomings, and gain insight into your abilities, moods, and tendencies. As you begin to work on building more Self-Awareness, here are three reflection exercises to get you started.

Harvesting: Reaping Lessons from Past Experiences

Think about significant experiences in your life that have caused you to reflect, take stock, and arrive at a higher level of self-understanding. What events, situations, hardships, or assignments stand out? In which experiences did you learn the most about yourself? Which ones showcased your strengths? Or uncovered weaknesses you weren't previously aware of? When did seeking feedback from others help you learn about yourself? And what did you do with that increased self-understanding?

Perhaps you didn't realize their significance at the time, but you recognize now how pivotal the experiences were in encouraging you to incorporate feedback you receive from others, enhancing your ability to learn from mistakes, and shaping your sense of self.

> "When you know better you do better."
>
> – Maya Angelou

Exercise 1

Draw your own time line of key experiences that caused you to pause and do some self-reflection. These may have been instances where you received surprising feedback, made a mistake, or learned something new.

For each key experience on your time line, take a moment to describe what happened. Then describe what you took away from that experience.

What was the situation? What did you do and why?

What did you take away from that experience? Do those lessons have any earmarks of Self-Awareness?

How have you applied what you learned to other situations?

Learning in Real-Time: Extracting Lessons from Current Experiences

Think about current projects you are on, struggles you are experiencing, changes that you are going through in your life or career. How are these experiences exciting or how are they causing angst for you? Perhaps you are struggling with some strong feelings, maybe you need clarity before making a decision, or maybe you've received some constructive feedback that was difficult to hear and has given you pause.

Exercise 2

"I've learned that I still have a lot to learn."

– Maya Angelou

Describe two or three current experiences which are ripe for extracting lessons and principles about self-reflection, seeking feedback, or being honest with yourself and others about your strengths and weaknesses.

Make a note of what you are learning from each experience (here and now) to take with you into future situations.

What is the situation? How are you approaching it, and why are you taking that approach?

What lessons are beginning to emerge from this experience?

How might these lessons benefit you in the future?

Anticipating: Thoughtfully Planning for Future Experiences and Lessons

If you've decided that it would be to your advantage to build Self-Awareness, it's time to think ahead. By understanding yourself and your impact on others, you will enhance your effectiveness in both your personal and professional life. How do you go about building Self-Awareness? Do you wait for situations to happen or hardships to test your agility? Not necessarily. While some situations are out of your control (you can still learn from these), there are many valuable experiences you can proactively seek out.

Experiences that build Self-Awareness are situations that are challenging—whether it's because they are emotionally laden; require new skills; have complex, interpersonal dynamics; or highlight some dissonance between your beliefs and your actions. Assignments that, in order to succeed, force you to be honest with yourself and candid with others about your shortcomings. These experiences help develop the ability to reflect and gain a clearer understanding of what you're good at and not so good at. And if the not so good is standing between you and your goals, doing something about it. These are actions of a self-aware leader.

Exercise 3

What is your goal? What is the result that you are looking for? How will building Self-Awareness help you achieve your goal? What does success look like?

Choose a few experiences that you would like to seek out in order to improve your Self-Awareness. These could be situations that are on the job or off the job, may be a part-time exploratory project, or a new full-time job that requires you to change departments, companies, or even relocate. Adjust the intensity-dial up or down depending on the size of the gap you are looking to close, the stage you're at in your career, and the level of challenge you are ready for.

Experiences to Sharpen Your Self-Awareness

Risk everything and take on a new role

Potential Features

Embracing new challenges

Encountering situations and problems never dealt with before

Learning the ropes in an unfamiliar setting or field

Some Examples

Move to a new city

Study something new and switch careers

Leave a secure job and volunteer for a tough or risky job in a different part of the business

Possible Lessons to Watch For

When you put yourself in new contexts, you learn more about who you are and how you can improve

Work outside of your home country and culture

Potential Features

Working in an unfamiliar culture or region

Learning a new language

Navigating new norms and rules

Some Examples

Take a rotational assignment to live and work abroad

Interview customers from different regions of the world

Manage a virtual, multicultural team that is dispersed around the globe

Deal with contrasting and conflicting aspects of multiple cultures and the subsequent culture shock

Possible Lessons to Watch For

Viewing yourself in the context of others and how others see you helps you make adjustments that are appropriate for the situation, context, and person

Start something new and unique for you, your company, or customers

Potential Features

Starting something from scratch

Building a new department, brand, or business unit

Establishing a new location or new region

Launching a new product or service

Introducing new systems, processes, or programs to all or part of the organization

Some Examples

Get seed funding for a new idea or venture

Navigate government regulation, negotiate with unions, or handle other complications on the path to a successful launch

Forge a new team

Possible Lessons to Watch For

By listening to criticism and feedback, you become aware of new considerations and learn to make quick adjustments

Take a job so complex that it makes your head spin

Potential Features

Dialing up the scope of your work and dealing with competing demands for your time

Increasing your visibility and responsibility

Taking on something that is outside your area of expertise

Handling complexity, uncertainty, and variety

Some Examples

Take a job that requires wearing multiple hats

Manage a team for the first time

Move to a new organization or relocate to a new region

Possible Lessons to Watch For

Once you become aware of your personal limits, you can find ways to work around them

Move to the field if you're at corporate (or vice versa)

Potential Features

Depending on other people to get your job done

Gaining perspective by being in a different part of the business

Some Examples

Manage product life cycle soup to nuts

Do a rotation in company planning

Do a rotation in sales

Possible Lessons to Watch For

Taking a new role in a different part of the business serves as a reminder of how much you have to learn from other people

Learn something new

Potential Features

Building new skills and expertise

Filling in gaps or updating an existing skill set

Being a student

Some Examples

Shadow an expert in your field of interest

Take an online course

Participate in leadership development courses at your company

Start working toward a new degree

Possible Lessons to Watch For

By formally studying a topic and taking time to reflect, you are more aware of what you know and what you don't know

Get involved outside of work

Potential Features

Pursuing new activities

Balancing work life with personal interests

Giving back to the community

Some Examples

Coach a sports team

Make peace with someone you disagree with or don't get along with very well

Volunteer for a nonprofit organization or cause

Try a new hobby or interest

Possible Lessons to Watch For

Seeing yourself in different contexts adds complexity and nuance to your identity

Teach others   **Potential Features**

Sharing what you know

Helping others acquire new knowledge and skills

Some Examples

Train customers or fellow employees

Design and teach a course

Coach or mentor someone

Seek informal feedback or formal evaluations from students

Possible Lessons to Watch For

Teaching others makes you more conscious of your own knowledge, skills, and approach

Whether you seek out a special project or whether you see the chance to change careers, taking on experiences that encourage reflection and require you to take a hard look at yourself will build Self-Awareness. These experiences might help you recognize the value of feedback, understand the source of your emotional reactions, and get in tune with opportunities for growth. If you are motivated to continue building your own Self-Awareness, here is what you can do:

Seek out experiences that challenge you to learn new things, seek feedback, and be candid about your strengths and weaknesses. Through these experiences, you will learn ways to reflect and gain insight that will serve you in future endeavors.

Extract key lessons and principles that will inspire you to dive deeper, analyze, discern, and encourage you to pursue additional personal development.

Use those insights in other situations as much as possible.

"Being true to the person you were created to be means accepting your faults as well as using your strengths. Accepting your shadow side is an essential part of being authentic. The problem comes down when people are so eager to win the approval of others that they try to cover their shortcomings and sacrifice their authenticity to gain the respect and admiration of their associates."

– Bill George

Learning Agility Factor

The extent to which an individual embraces complexity, examines problems in unique and unusual ways, is inquisitive, and can make fresh connections between different concepts

Mental Agility

Agility

Making Fresh Connections

Mental Agility:
Making Fresh Connections

To be mentally agile is to be drawn toward newness and complexity. It is the ability to be mentally quick, to delve deeply and thoroughly analyze problems, and to find parallels and contrasts that inform fresh thinking. Mental Agility is exemplified in a curious, inquisitive, and analytical nature in the search for meaning.

Examples

Approaching the world with curiosity

Making connections that prove difficult for others

Searching for deeper meaning

Simplifying the complex so others can also grasp it

Solving problems by applying deep analysis and fresh perspective

Helping others think things through

Seeing many parts of something while simultaneously divining its essence

Do you find yourself in awe when people solve a difficult issue or problem that you were convinced was unsolvable? Not only did they solve the problem, but they exhibited the kind of boundless curiosity that compelled them to ask the question in the first place. Some people thrive on exploring alternatives, finding hidden connections, or surfacing an unconventional point of view. You can't always see it, but you sense that they are doing mental gymnastics with ideas—flipping puzzle pieces around, viewing problems from every angle, all with tremendous flexibility that makes it look effortless.

Galileo Galilei was one such mental gymnast. His contributions in the fields of astronomy, physics, mathematics, and philosophy earned him the title "Father of Modern Science." In addition to his discoveries, the experimental methods and ways of thinking he employed were also significant. Galileo made connections between seemingly unrelated disciplines, which helped him adopt an integrated approach to tackling various theoretical questions. He tuned out established authorities and sought to observe scientific and mathematical phenomena from

fresh perspectives and through experimentation. He used visual thought experiments, bringing his scientific theories to life for his readers. In one case, he asked readers to consider this: If two people are playing catch inside the cabin of a smooth-sailing ship, they can throw the ball back and forth with the same effort that it takes on land, regardless of the speed or direction of the ship.

Like Galileo, mentally agile people help other people think things through and make the complex simple. They have a knack for diving into the complexity of a problem, getting to the essence, and articulating the solution with simplicity and elegance. Though it may seem counterintuitive, it is because they understand the problem so completely that they can articulate it so simply and elegantly for others to understand. Often, their breakthroughs come from having broad interests and a curious, questioning mind-set.

Galileo Galilei

Steve Jobs is another example of Mental Agility. Like Galileo, Jobs made connections—fresh connections—not obvious to others. Much of what is now common in the marketplace and emblematic of the Apple® brand is, at its essence, a marriage between two unlikely bedfellows: technology and humanities. How did Jobs bring this juxtaposition in problem solving to life? One example is how he approached design. Jobs knew that in order to sell more computers, he needed to make them accessible. He took technology devices that were potentially intimidating and made them user-friendly by eliminating all extraneous buttons, trays, and keypads and adding features like handles, colors, and a screen that resembled a face. His ability to connect seemingly disparate things was a hallmark of his innovations: combining the aesthetics of calligraphy with computer interface; turning a prank or a whim (a blue box that made free long-distance calls) into a commercial product. The famous "Think Different" marketing campaign reflected how he approached inventing new products with his team.

Steve Jobs

Galileo Galilei and Steve Jobs are archetypes of Mental Agility, but how did they become such adept, tireless, and creative problem solvers? Agile thinkers are often curious and energized by what others might characterize as intellectual tangents. They dabble in multiple disciplines, often irritating established experts by their willingness to question, challenge, and flaunt conventional thinking. They have a comfort with ambiguity, a speed with which they shift gears, and an ability to juggle many ideas simultaneously that can have a dizzying effect on those around them. They combine different ideas, play with combinations, and cut to the core in ways that are not always transparent to the onlooker. What could you learn if you were to explore the experiences that shaped the ability to think this way? Could you seek out similar experiences that would enhance your thinking—make you curious and nimble?

"Simple can be harder than complex: You have to work hard to get your thinking clean to make it simple. But it's worth it in the end because once you get there, you can move mountains."

– Steve Jobs
(From *BusinessWeek* interview, May 1998)

"To raise new questions, new possibilities, to regard old problems from a new angle, requires creative imagination and marks real advance in science."

Albert Einstein – German-born American physicist and Nobel Prize winner

Becoming Mentally Agile – Albert Einstein

Let's take a deeper look at the experiences that contributed to inquisitive and nimble thinking in another famous example of Mental Agility: Albert Einstein. Einstein's image has become synonymous with genius—something most people would not even consider aspiring to. Yet, history tells a more complex and nuanced story of how Einstein's life and experiences shaped his ability to generate profound breakthroughs. And it turns out IQ was not necessarily the distinguishing characteristic. Einstein had a tendency to reject conformity and, instead, question conventional ways of thinking. This behavior did not endear Einstein to his professors. Indeed, throughout his schooling, Einstein was not at the top of his class. Operating outside of the academic mainstream, Einstein's first dissertations were a departure from established theories and were swiftly rejected by the established scientific community.

Apt to suspend reality in the course of his exploratory thought experiments, Einstein entertained arguments and followed their logical paths without the foundational principles first being proven or established. He had a boyish sense of wonder about the universe as well as everyday objects—never bored by things others might view as mundane. Einstein wrestled with the "great eternal riddle" he saw all around him. His curiosity led him to appreciate music, philosophy, mathematics, and science, and his interdisciplinary interests informed his worldview and approach. Diving into complex problems, he would find principles or parallels and visualize images that evoked his theories, such as falling through an elevator shaft or riding alongside a light beam.

Einstein viewed his intuition and intellectual ability as the culmination of previous experiences. His grounding in and knowledge of theoretical physics was a major and obvious source of his ability to generate breakthroughs. But what were the experiences that influenced *how* Einstein approached problems? What key events guided and shaped his ability to take complex and ambiguous questions and do the mental gymnastics that resulted in breakthrough insight?

Building
Mental Agility

Albert Einstein's Experiences

1885
Einstein's mother arranges
for him to take violin lessons

Einstein's mother was an accomplished pianist and instilled in him a love of classical music. When she encouraged him to learn the violin, Einstein bristled at the obligatory practice time, but soon music became another way for him to ponder the mysteries of the universe. Mozart in particular resonated with Einstein's developing belief in the harmony, elegance, and beauty of the universe. Often, he immersed himself in playing music when he needed time to reflect or solve problems. His son Hans Albert remembered, "Whenever he felt that he had come to the end of the road or faced a difficult challenge in his work, he would take refuge in music, and that would solve all his difficulties." Likewise, a friend relayed, "He would often play his violin in his kitchen late at night, improvising melodies while he pondered complicated problems. Then, suddenly, in the middle of playing, he would announce excitedly, 'I've got it!' As if by inspiration, the answer to the problem would have come to him in the midst of music."

Small Experiences – Big Lessons

Not all lessons come from monumental or arduous situations. Sometimes a brief encounter brings lasting insight. Many of Einstein's small experiences accumulated into foundational principles for how he thought about the world and approached solving problems. Highlighted on these pages are a few that contributed to his ability to be curious and analytical, get to the essence of a problem, and find meaning.

The harmony in the music reflects the harmony of the universe

All great beauty is pure simplicity

Taking time to reflect can foster breakthroughs

These lessons build breadth, the ability to reflect, and the inclination to allow diverse interests to cross-pollinate.

1895
Works at family-owned electrical supply company

Throughout the spring and summer of 1895, Einstein worked in the family business—an electrical supply company—where he mastered the technology and mechanics of generating electricity. He helped his Uncle Jakob refine calculations for a new machine and how the coils and magnets moved in the generator. Later that summer, he went on to write an essay about "how an electric current sets the surrounding ether in a kind of momentary motion." A complex idea which he succinctly articulated in 14 handwritten paragraphs. In the paper, he made suggestions about additional experiments that could explain how a magnetic field forms around electric current. While working in the family business furthered his thinking, he preferred not to focus his intellect on practical business matters. Einstein wrote to a friend, "I was originally supposed to become an engineer, but the thought of having to expend my creative energy on things that make practical, everyday life even more refined, with a bleak capital gain as the goal, was unbearable to me. Thinking for its own sake, like music!"

Hands-on experiences can spark new theories

Writing and explaining a theory can help make complex concepts more simple and accessible

Intellectual pursuits trump business pursuits for those not motivated by practical life and wealth

These lessons develop the ability to get at root causes, to help others with problem solving, and to express complex ideas in simple, easy-to-understand ways.

Compass
One day when Einstein was sick in bed, his father brought him a compass. Einstein was enthralled that the needle was not moved by some mechanical method, but by some deeply hidden and mysterious force. The compass propelled his sense of wonder and curiosity that led to his dedication to field theories—how gravity and electromagnetic fields are forces that affect matter and other fields. "I can still remember—or at least I believe I can remember—that this experience made a deep and lasting impression on me. Something deeply hidden had to be behind things."

Underlying, mysterious forces influence the movement of things

Translation to Mental Agility:
Curiosity and wonder fuel the motivation to delve deeply into problems and questions.

Exhausted and limited by the tightly controlled learning environment in his school, Einstein left school and declared to his parents that he was never going back to Germany. Einstein enrolled in a prep school in Aarau, Switzerland, which was based on the philosophy of Swiss education reformer Johann Heinrich Pestalozzi, whose motto was "Learning by head, hand, and heart." Pedagogical principles included respect for students; freedom of thought; encouraging students to visualize images and conduct thought experiments; and challenging students to question, formulate new hypotheses, and reach their own conclusions. This freedom of thought and mutual respect between teacher and student created an environment that made a big impression on Einstein. Free action and personal responsibility became his preferred modus operandi as opposed to relying on outward authority. It was here that he began to noodle on the visual thought experiment that would culminate in the theory of relativity years later: picturing what it would be like to ride alongside a light beam. Visualizing thought experiments became a central strategy for problem solving in Einstein's career.

Geometry

Early intellectual exercises in applied mathematics gave Einstein an appreciation for finding answers through reasoning. Einstein took delight in hunting for unknown variables. Geometry provided the opportunity to prove theorems by looking for similarities across figures and relying on established principles to arrive at a new conclusion. Reflecting on this experience Einstein relates, "As a boy of 12, I was thrilled to see that it was possible to find out truth by reasoning alone, without the help of any outside experience. I became more and more convinced that nature could be understood as a relatively simple mathematical structure."

New discoveries can be made through reasoning and by finding what unifies seemingly separate things

Translation to Mental Agility:
Contrasts, parallels, and unique combinations can reveal connections between seemingly unrelated things.

Asking new questions is more intellectually rewarding than regurgitating old answers

Visualizing a question or problem makes it possible to consider multiple variables simultaneously and determine the essence of the problem

Thought experiments are a way to delve deeply into a problem and find meaning beneath the surface

These lessons develop the ability to look at problems from different angles, find solutions without oversimplifying, and the patience to wrestle with contradictions.

1902
Finds work at a patent office in Bern

Rejected by numerous professors in his quest to find an assistant professor position, Einstein was grateful to secure a job in a patent office. When an acquaintance complained aloud that work in the patent office was boring, Einstein told another friend, "Certain people find everything boring." Instead, he found the applications for patents that came across his desk "uncommonly diversified" and interesting. Each day, Einstein was able to complete his job duties within a few hours and was afforded time to work at his desk on his other pursuits. Now that he was outside of academia, he had the freedom to think up unconventional theories and write controversial papers. He was not beholden to an institution and could comfortably challenge established thinkers and theories of the day. Einstein's boss appreciated that he was rebellious and creative. He instructed Einstein, "You have to remain critically vigilant. When you pick up an application, think that everything the inventor says is wrong."

Access to a variety of ideas and inventions provides fodder in unexpected ways

Being outside of the establishment affords a new perspective, an opportunity to question past solutions, and a willingness to challenge assumptions

Challenge conventional wisdom, even if everyone else thinks it's established truth

These lessons build breadth of knowledge and experience as well as a healthy skepticism and willingness to question authority and challenge assumptions.

Explosion

A Zurich Polytechnic professor of physics, Jean Pernet, noted Einstein's unconventional methods in his physics practicum. One day in the lab, an explosion injured Einstein's right hand and required him to get stitches at the clinic. Writing and playing violin had to be put on hold for weeks. After the accident he was, understandably, much less interested in conducting lab experiments. Without access to particle accelerators and other advanced technology, his theories couldn't be tested in a lab, anyway. In the end, Einstein's preference for thought experiments suited the complex theoretical problems he was solving.

Theoretical experiments are as interesting as lab experiments, and much safer

Translation to Mental Agility:
The mind can be used as a scientific lab, using inquiry and logic to analyze complex problems.

*"A new idea comes suddenly
and in a rather intuitive way.
But intuition is nothing but the outcome
of earlier intellectual experience."*

– Albert Einstein

Experiences
for building your
Mental Agility

Einstein's Lessons Influenced His Approach to His Work

> "People like you and me never grow old. We never cease to stand like curious children before the great mystery into which we were born."
>
> – Albert Einstein in a letter to a friend

Einstein recognized that his earlier experiences influenced his intuition and discovery of special relativity and, later, general relativity. From his experiences in school in Germany and his lessons in philosophy, he brought a healthy skepticism and rebelliousness which led him to question established authority and theories. Learning to conduct visual thought experiments in school in Aarau led him to ask the question about what it would be like to ride at the speed of light alongside a light beam. His lessons in geometry reinforced the principle that one can find truth through reasoning. This led him to wrestle with his thought experiment for 10 years while trying to reconcile the conflict between Newton's law of mechanics and Maxwell's constancy of the speed of light. Finally, the lessons he learned by working on his uncle's generator and through his work at the Swiss patent office contributed to his ability to quickly grasp the essence of a problem.

Einstein's collected experiences—those sought out (a new school, a job in a patent office) and those placed before him (music lessons, a gift of a compass) all played a role in shaping how he thought about the world. His ability to reflect upon these experiences and benefit from the accumulated knowledge, wisdom, and principles they fostered furthered his ability to make such significant scientific contributions.

Building Mental Agility by Learning from Your Experiences

What connections can you make between Einstein's experiences and your own? What inspiration do you draw from his journey toward becoming mentally agile? Between past, present, and future, you may find that you have a strong starting point for discovering and developing your Mental Agility. Both on-the-job and off-the-job experiences can have a powerful hand in developing your drive to get things done in new and challenging situations. As you begin to work on building more Mental Agility, here are three reflection exercises to get you started.

Harvesting: Reaping Lessons from Past Experiences

Think about the significant experiences in your life that have inspired you to be curious, bring a fresh perspective to a complex problem, or help others think things through. What events, situations, hardships, or assignments stand out? In what circumstance did you have that "aha" moment where everything came into focus and the solution to a tough problem presented itself? When did being curious lead you to discover new ways of viewing things?

Exercise 1

Draw your own time line of key experiences that taught you about aspects of Mental Agility, such as integrating different perspectives, analyzing a complex problem, or getting to the root cause of an issue.

For each key experience on your time line, take a moment to describe what happened. Then describe what you took away from that experience.

What was the situation? What did you do and why?

What did you take away from that experience? Do those lessons have any earmarks of Mental Agility?

How have you applied what you learned to other situations?

"When forced to summarize the general theory of relativity in one sentence: Time and space and gravitation have no separate existence from matter."

– Albert Einstein

Learning in Real-Time: Extracting Lessons from Current Experiences

Think about current projects you are on, struggles you are experiencing, changes that you are going through in your life or career. How are these experiences exciting or how are they causing angst for you? Maybe you are sifting through a complex problem trying to find the nuggets of meaning, maybe you are on the verge of an inspired idea that marries the best of two worlds, or maybe you found yourself wondering why and you are indulging your curiosity.

Exercise 2

Describe two or three current experiences which are ripe for extracting lessons and principles about aspects of Mental Agility, such as curiosity, analytical thinking, and looking at things differently.

Make a note of what you are learning from each experience (here and now) to take with you into future situations.

What is the situation? How are you approaching it, and why are you taking that approach?

What lessons are beginning to emerge from this experience?

How might these lessons benefit you in the future?

Anticipating: Thoughtfully Planning for Future Experiences and Lessons

If you've decided that it would be to your advantage to build Mental Agility, it's time to look ahead. How could behaviors such as cognitive flexibility, analytical thinking, and problem solving be advantageous to you and help you achieve your personal and career goals? Where can you continue building Mental Agility? Do you wait for situations to happen or hardships to test your agility? Not necessarily. While some situations are out of your control (you can still learn from these), there are many valuable experiences you can proactively seek out.

Experiences that build Mental Agility are situations that challenge your assumptions, expand your perspective, and increase the cognitive load you can carry. Assignments that force you to analyze or evaluate a strategic approach, solve a conundrum, generate viable alternatives to the status quo, or figure out something when you don't have all the information. These experiences help develop cognitive flexibility, tolerance for ambiguity, the ability to embrace complexity, and the clarity of thought to articulate ideas elegantly. These are the qualities of a mentally agile person.

Exercise 3

What is your goal? What is the result that you are looking for?
How will building Mental Agility help you achieve your goal?
What does success look like?

Choose a few experiences that you would like to seek out
in order to improve your Mental Agility. These could be situations
that are on the job or off the job, may be a part-time exploratory project,
or a new full-time job that requires you to change departments, companies,
or even relocate. Adjust the intensity-dial up or down depending on the
size of the gap you are looking to close, the stage you're at in your
career, and the level of challenge you are ready for.

Experiences to Sharpen Your Mental Agility

Lead a project team

Potential Features

Managing competing priorities—too many objectives with limited resources

Learning something on the fly

Getting other people's ideas to come together under a tight deadline

Integrating individual pieces into a whole picture

Some Examples

Head up a cross-department strategic initiative

Coordinate an election campaign

Organize a family reunion

Direct a play or chair an event-planning committee

Possible Lessons to Watch For

Getting to the core of an issue and setting priorities are key when under the gun

Take responsibility for delivering a viable business strategy

Potential Features

Pressing forward despite a lack of information and resources

Creating a strategy that will make a business venture profitable

Charting new ground in a high-stakes market

Some Examples

Sit on an advisory board for a community organization

Commercialize a new product

Present an idea to the leadership team

Possible Lessons to Watch For

One way to road test a strategy is to look for parallels in different industries or disciplines and play things out through logic and reason

Start something new and unique for you, your company, or customers

Potential Features

Starting something from scratch

Building a new department, brand, or business unit

Establishing a new location or new region

Launching a new product or service

Introducing new systems, processes, or programs to all or part of the organization

Some Examples

Identify an unmet need and design something that would fill the gap

Oversee the adoption of a new process or system

Find a way to create a spin-off of a successful product

Possible Lessons to Watch For

Resistance can either be a bellwether for a bad idea or a sign that the idea is inspired—the trick is figuring out which

Risk everything and take on a new role

Potential Features

Embracing new challenges

Encountering situations and problems never dealt with before

Learning the ropes in an unfamiliar setting or field

Some Examples

Work for a new boss or on a new team

Move from doing the work to managing people who do the work

Take a job in a different division or company

Leave a job you love to take a chance on something new

Possible Lessons to Watch For

Tackling new problems opens your mind in ways you could never imagine and gives you a broader perspective than you had before

Turn around a business or product that is in a downward spiral

Potential Features

Going against the odds to deliver a tough project on time and on budget

Making tough decisions (trade-offs) that impact a variety of people

Some Examples

Solve a problem that requires you to think creatively

Conduct a comprehensive assessment of a struggling business

Take a floundering product and retrofit it

Lead others through a turnaround strategy in an uncertain and pressure-filled business climate

Possible Lessons to Watch For

Looking for breakthroughs in unexpected places

Take a job so complex that it makes your head spin

Potential Features

Dialing up the scope of your work and dealing with competing demands for your time

Increasing your visibility and responsibility

Taking on something that is outside your area of expertise

Handling complexity, uncertainty, and variety

Some Examples

Switch to a new function, industry, or business

Manage a project with a multitude of interdependencies

Take on new responsibilities without giving up former responsibilities

Possible Lessons to Watch For

When you have many things going on at once, often the ideas and solutions cross-pollinate

Take on an individual project

Potential Features

Choosing to take responsibility for a project you feel passionate about

Making a contribution where you see a need

Some Examples

Do a review of a completed project to analyze what went well and what didn't

Conduct and analyze a survey

Identify something that needs improvement and make it your pet project

Lobby the government on behalf of a cause

Possible Lessons to Watch For

By taking the time to reflect and get a fresh perspective, you can find new ways to solve problems

Expand your perspective

Potential Features

Having conversations with people who have different perspectives than you do

Reading about an unfamiliar topic

Some Examples

Study a new trend

Do a job swap

Interview people outside your company or field

Analyze the competition

Possible Lessons to Watch For

When you know a little bit, you become curious to know more and it sparks so many questions

Big and small experiences. Events outside of your control. Assignments you seek out. All of these have the potential to produce moments of clarity and inspiration when you pause to reflect on lessons learned. These experiences might spark your curiosity, fuel breakthroughs in thinking, help you find parallels and contrasts, and cause you to delve deeply into complex problems, emerging with elegant solutions. Or you may just find joy in exploring something new and unfamiliar. If you are motivated to continue building your own Mental Agility, here is what you can do:

Seek out experiences that challenge you to think from a new perspective, integrate ideas, or deal with complexity.

Extract key lessons and principles that will help you frame your analytic approach and mental models.

Use those insights in other situations as much as possible.

"Here's to the crazy ones.

The misfits. The rebels. The troublemakers.

The round pegs in the square holes.

The ones who see things differently."

(From the poem featured in Apple's
"Think Different" marketing campaign)

The degree to which one is open-minded toward others, enjoys interacting with a diversity of people, understands their unique strengths, interests, and limitations, and uses them effectively to accomplish organizational goals

People Agility

Bringing Out the Best in Others

People Agility:
Bringing Out the Best in Others

People Agility is the ability to relate well to others—taking a flexible approach, depending on the person or the situation. People agile individuals listen, understand, and empathize with others. Open-minded toward people and situations, they are willing to shift their perspective or position. They bring out the best in others and can get things done through other people. And, depending on the situation, they exhibit appropriate lightheartedness.

Examples

Relating well to all kinds of people

Getting things done through others

Navigating both interpersonal and political dynamics

Listening and understanding others' points of view

Adjusting style and approach for different people

Dealing with conflict in a way that doesn't burn bridges

"The roles we play in each other's lives are only as powerful as the trust and connection between us—the protection, safety, and caring we are willing to share."

– Oprah Winfrey

Have you noticed how some people exude genuine empathy as they relate to others? All other distractions fall away as they focus on listening and understanding in a way that makes people open up and feel valued. Not only are they at ease in a variety of situations with different kinds of people, but they can adjust their style and demeanor for the situation. Being so in tune with others helps them bring out the best in people.

Oprah Winfrey is masterful at this. Winfrey built an influential media empire not only due to a shrewd business sense, but also because of her ability to genuinely relate to and build a warm rapport with her guests and her audience. The connection she makes through her interactions has transformed the talk-show genre. So captivated are her audiences that she is able to influence what they read, what they eat, what they buy—a phenomenon referred to as the "Oprah Effect." This relational connection has also advanced philanthropic efforts. On one show, Winfrey's appeal for children in Africa prompted viewers to donate over $7 million. All told, her former charity, Oprah's Angel Network, raised more than $80 million for charitable projects.

Empathizing and bringing out the best in other people are aspects of People Agility. But People Agility also

Oprah Winfrey

involves being able to handle tension, conflict, or disagreement in a calm and respectful way. Having the patience and composure to understand different positions while keeping an open mind. Building trust among key decision makers, stakeholders, or team members. Giving credit more than taking credit. All of the above are marks of a people agile leader.

Martti Ahtisaari, the former president of Finland, won the Nobel Peace Prize in 2008 for his ability to bring opposing factions together, resolve conflict, and negotiate peace agreements in places like Namibia, Kosovo, Indonesia, and Northern Ireland. In his role as mediator, Ahtisaari recognizes the importance of engaging with all sides and gaining an understanding of their grievances and

Martti Ahtisaari

arguments. He deals constructively with all parties, even when he disagrees with their positions. Recognizing that conflict resolution is a matter of cooperation and partnership, he discourages people from viewing him, the outside mediator, as the catalyst; rather, he shares responsibility and credit for the peace that is achieved.

Oprah Winfrey and Martti Ahtisaari are two examples of people agile leaders. Both recognize the importance of demonstrating that they value people. Both understand how, by building relationships, they can meet their objectives. But how did they become so astute in this area? Let's take a look at some formative experiences that develop this ability. Wisdom gained and lessons learned from experiences shape a person's ability to receive and affect other people with lightness and grace.

"All conflicts can be resolved. Wars and conflicts are not inevitable. They are caused by human beings. There are always interests that are furthered by war. Therefore those who have power and influence can also stop them. Peace is a question of will."

– Martti Ahtisaari

"Don't address their brains. Address their hearts."

Nelson Mandela – Former South African president

Becoming People Agile – Nelson Mandela

Let's take a deeper look at an individual who had a long journey toward becoming a people agile leader who could reconcile enemies: Nelson Mandela. Born Rolihlahla Mandela, meaning "troublemaker," he was an anti-apartheid activist who, as a young man, lost hope in the pacifist approach to negotiating with White South Africans. Mandela received military training abroad and established the military wing of the African National Congress (ANC) in 1961. As a liberation fighter, Mandela was a force to be reckoned with, but later in life, he became a force for reconciliation and healing for his nation as South Africa's first Black president.

What prompted Mandela's shift from liberation fighter to masterful negotiator able to influence an entire nation? His transformation seems to have come to fruition in a most unlikely place: prison. A prime example of this shift relates to Mandela's dealings with South Africa's minister of justice, Kobie Coetsee. Coetsee was instructed to begin talks with Mandela. In the very same month as the Geneva Summit meeting between U.S. president Ronald Reagan (another example of People Agility) and Soviet leader Mikhail Gorbachev, Mandela employed a similar amicable, charming, dignified, and respectful demeanor in the first critical meeting with Coetsee. With Mandela still imprisoned, the relaxed exchange built rapport and signaled the beginning of a new era dominated by diplomacy and relationship building.

What key experiences provided the foundation for Mandela's ability to become open-minded, deal constructively with conflict, and effectively relate to those who opposed him and his ideas? A look at the wisdom and lessons Mandela took from a few key experiences sheds light on his transformation into the unifying leader he became.

Building
People Agility
Nelson Mandela's Experiences

1927
Father died and he went to
live with Chief Jongintaba

When Mandela lost his father at a young age, he went to live with his father's friend, Chief Jongintaba. It was here that Mandela learned the history and tradition of the Xhosa nation, Mandela's ancestral people. He was introduced to the philosophy of *ubuntu*, the idea that one's humanity is derived from how one relates to other people. Chief Jongintaba was frequently called upon to act as a justice. Tribesmen would present their grievances, and Mandela watched as Jongintaba would listen without interrupting and seek consensus among the disagreeing parties. Mandela admired Jongintaba's self-control and fairness, and many years later sought to emulate his early mentor.

Small Experiences – Big Lessons

Many of Mandela's other experiences refined his approach to relating to all kinds of people. Highlighted on these pages are a few experiences that contributed to Mandela influencing others and bringing out the best in people under difficult circumstances.

People have a right to be heard

Conflict can be resolved with dignity and fairness

Listening is a powerful tool for a leader

These lessons build conflict management skills.

1938
Elected to his university's student council

After graduating from high school, Mandela enrolled in Fort Hare, a small college with only 150 students. Founded by White missionaries in 1916, it was the only Black university in South Africa. Two issues sparked Mandela's debut in politics at Fort Hare. First, he sought fair representation for freshman students on the student council. Second, he felt strongly that the student council should have a greater sway with the administration of the school, particularly regarding the quality of the food served. But the administration was silent on these demands and student committee elections proceeded with only 25 students voting. Mandela, along with five of his peers, was elected to the Student Representative Council, but Mandela refused to accept his post under the conditions and wrote a letter of resignation to the principal. The principal threatened Mandela with expulsion. Chief Jongintaba urged Mandela to go back to the principal and apologize. Feeling compelled to make a stand on moral grounds, Mandela refused to apologize, left school, and made the difficult decision to abandon his adoptive father and benefactor.

Standing up for fairness and democracy can be costly

Engaging with opponents when both parties are stubborn can have an undesirable result

These lessons plant the seeds for how critical it is to work with key decision makers in a way that results in a positive outcome for both parties.

Law firm
In November 1952, Mandela and his friend Oliver Tambo opened South Africa's first Black law firm. As a courtroom attorney, Mandela made compelling arguments appealing to logic, reason, and a sense of moral right and wrong. The casework was often focused on fighting injustice and reflected the reality of the time. According to Mandela, throughout trials, including his own, "We used the courtroom as a platform to address the country and the world." Legal discourse became a key instrument in Mandela's ability to reason with and influence fellow countrymen, prison guards, and political leaders.

Using logic and reason is one way to fight for what's right

Translation to People Agility:
Presenting ideas and arguments in the language of the target audience can plant seeds of persuasion.

Boxing

In part, Mandela's amateur boxing career was a way to blow off steam. The demands of his professional, political, and family life were stressful, and boxing was an escape. He was drawn to the sport, not for its violent display, but for its strategy. He appreciated the rhythm in the ring, the exchange of punches, the timing, the footwork. In many ways, boxing became a metaphor which Mandela drew upon in his interpersonal dealings—staying light and flexible, knowing when to hold back and wait, knowing when to make a move.

Staying in tune with your opponent can inform your strategy

Translation to People Agility:
Making quick and accurate judgments about people, reading their responses, and strategically planning the interaction to achieve a desired result.

1964-1982
Dedicated to understanding and relating to his captors on Robben Island

Sentenced to life in prison for treason in 1964, Mandela would spend nearly three decades in jail, isolated from his family and the world. The first 18 years he spent on Robben Island were under brutal conditions. In addition to continuing his legal studies, Mandela studied his captors and how to influence them in respectful, nonconfrontational ways. He studied their language (Afrikaans), their history (including the Anglo-Boer wars), and honed interpersonal and negotiation tactics that eventually led to better conditions and treatment. He worked to manage his emotions, particularly his anger. He observed how prison guards responded when he treated them as equals—with courtesy and respect. One small but impactful gesture—Mandela would often share vegetables with the guards from a small patch of land he was allowed to cultivate. Honing this interpersonal statesmanship was not in vain. Mandela called upon the calm, open-minded, mutually respectful demeanor he had carefully cultivated when he wrote to the minister of justice proposing a dialogue regarding his future and the future of South Africa.

Learning about the other person's point of view builds rapport

Treating oppressors like humans can prompt them to return the respect

Framing ideas in a way the recipient can relate to is more effective

These lessons develop open-mindedness, the ability to see things from another point of view, and mutual respect toward others, even those who are enemies.

1964-1982
Mediated conflicts between prisoners and guards on Robben Island

Life in prison with about 30 African National Congress (ANC) comrades prompted an organizational structure to keep some political cohesion and activism alive. Mandela headed up the organization, which served to provide political education for prisoners, escalate issues to prison authorities, and decide on negotiation tactics. The ANC was not the only political faction present, and eventually Mandela and others persuaded the other groups to set up a joint committee that would act on behalf of all prisoners. Later, when a new and more militant generation of fighters were incarcerated at Robben Island, Mandela often mediated between the guards and the prisoners. Prisoners who had strong and opposing views came to respect Mandela for his leadership and ability to navigate the political waters of the prison system.

Calm, collective action yields desired results

Carefully gauging other people's responses allows the opportunity to make adjustments in negotiation tactics

By taking cues from the situation rather than emotions, you are better able to self-manage and lead productively

These lessons build political astuteness, flexibility, collaboration, composure, and influencing skills.

Adversary turned supporter
In 1970, Colonel Piet Badenhorst became commanding officer of the Robben Island prison. Badenhorst was particularly threatening and punitive. In a hearing about harsh treatment, when Badenhorst publicly threatened Mandela in front of the judge, Mandela reasoned with the judge, "If he can threaten me here, in your presence, you can imagine what he does when you are not here." Badenhorst was removed from his post, but not before pulling Mandela aside privately and saying, "I just want to wish you people good luck." In that simple exchange, Mandela was shocked to witness the transformation of the callous oppressor into a polite supporter.

People are not one-dimensional, evil figures; context influences behavior

Translation to People Agility:
Being open-minded toward others' experiences and points of view tailors communication and interpersonal interactions for the audience.

Barcelona Olympics

In 1992, Mandela attended the Olympic Games in Barcelona. At one point, he stood up and he could feel the entire stadium resounding with the enthusiasm of the crowd. For Mandela, this illustrated the power that sport had to move people emotionally. He relayed this experience to Francois Pienaar, the captain of the South African Springbok rugby team. A story popularized in the film *Invictus*, the rugby team became a focal point for unification. Mandela's goal: "Let us use sport for the purpose of nation-building and promoting all the ideas which we think will lead to peace and stability in our country."

Rooting for a common team can build solidarity and pride

Translation to People Agility:
Bringing out the best in others, helping them shine, and tapping into something that is important and emotional for them can have a unifying effect.

*"Know your enemy—
and learn about his favorite sport."*

– Nelson Mandela

Experiences
for building your
People Agility

Mandela's Lessons Influenced How He Approached His Work

Mandela may have been a natural leader from early in life, as some of his colleagues observed, but he gathered lessons from his experiences, which made him a people agile leader. Lessons learned from collective efforts over the years led him to regard the people of South Africa with gratitude and appreciation. Perspective gained from seeing guards adjust their demeanor led him to treat leaders in power and apartheid supporters with respect and understanding. His study of interpersonal relationships helped him change the minds and hearts of his previous oppressors. Recognizing the power in understanding others and building relationships, Mandela abandoned militancy and embraced diplomacy as the instrument that would unify a deeply divided nation.

Mandela is a model of People Agility. He brought out the best in other people by seeing their points of view, giving them the benefit of the doubt, and treating them with mutual respect. His authentic charm and warm demeanor put others at ease in even the most tense and controversial situations. Mandela became well respected by the very people who previously saw him as a terrorist. His composed dignity and diplomacy showed South Africans a new way forward as one nation.

Building People Agility by Learning from Your Experiences

What connections can you make between Mandela's experiences and your own? What inspiration do you draw from his journey toward becoming people agile? Between past, present, and future, you may find that you have a strong starting point for discovering and developing your People Agility. Both on-the-job and off-the-job experiences can help you develop your ability to flex your style to the situation, relate to your audience, and bring out the best in others. As you begin to work on building more People Agility, here are three reflection exercises to get you started.

Harvesting: Reaping Lessons from Past Experiences

Think about the significant experiences in your life that challenged you to relate to people. Maybe the situation required you to relate to your audience; have a calm demeanor in a tense, interpersonal situation; understand someone else's perspective; or to give credit and let others shine. What events, situations, hardships, or assignments stand out? What situations have led you to empathize with others? What circumstances have required you to keep an open mind to alternative points of view?

Exercise 1

Draw your own time line of key experiences that taught you about aspects of People Agility, such as building rapport, relating to people who see the world very differently from you, and constructively managing conflict.

For each key experience on your time line, take a moment to describe what happened. Then describe what you took away from that experience.

What was the situation? What did you do and why?

What did you take away from that experience? Do those lessons have any earmarks of People Agility?

How have you applied what you learned to other situations?

Learning in Real-Time: Extracting Lessons from Current Experiences

Think about current projects you are on, struggles you are experiencing, changes that you are going through in your life or career. How are these experiences exciting or how are they causing angst for you? Perhaps you are struggling to stay composed and objective in an interpersonal conflict, maybe you see the opportunity to be more open-minded and flexible, or maybe you see the opportunity to cultivate relationships with others.

Exercise 2

Describe two or three current experiences which are ripe for extracting lessons and principles about aspects of People Agility, such as reading people, adjusting your approach, defusing tension, and getting the best out of people.

Make a note of what you are learning from each experience (here and now) to take with you into future situations.

What is the situation? How are you approaching it, and why are you taking that approach?

What lessons are beginning to emerge from this experience?

How might these lessons benefit you in the future?

Anticipating: Thoughtfully Planning for Future Experiences and Lessons

If you've decided that it would be to your advantage to build People Agility, it's time to plan for the future. You see how behaviors such as managing conflict productively, staying flexible and open-minded, and cultivating the ability to relate to people will serve your personal and professional goals. How do you go about building People Agility? Do you wait for situations to happen or hardships to test your agility? Not necessarily. While some situations are out of your control (you can still learn from these), there are many valuable experiences you can proactively seek out.

Experiences that build People Agility are situations that demand seeing things from diverse points of view, navigating emotions and politics, and managing your reactions even when you feel strongly. Assignments that force you to deal with uncomfortable situations, reach consensus with opposing groups, and communicate with people in a way that speaks to them on many levels. These experiences help develop the interpersonal warmth and calm that can build bridges, with the potential to influence productive, collective efforts. These are qualities of a people agile leader.

Exercise 3

What is your goal? What is the result that you are looking for? How will building People Agility help you achieve your goal? What does success look like?

Choose a few experiences that you would like to seek out in order to improve your People Agility. These could be situations that are on the job or off the job, may be a part-time exploratory project, or a new full-time job that requires you to change departments, companies, or even relocate. Adjust the intensity-dial up or down depending on the size of the gap you are looking to close, the stage you're at in your career, and the level of challenge you are ready for.

Experiences to Sharpen Your People Agility

Lead a significant change effort	**Potential Features**
	Introducing a change that could meet a lot of resistance
	Getting buy-in and cooperation from others
	Juggling multiple stakeholders and decision makers
	Some Examples
	Lead the messaging and communications for a change initiative
	Facilitate a decision process that requires you to build consensus
	Advocate for a necessary but unpopular change
	Possible Lessons to Watch For
	Being open-minded and empathetic can facilitate adoption of a change

Solve a crisis for people

Potential Features

Leading others during an unpredictable and scary time

Being a spokesperson to the company and the public; enduring intense scrutiny and criticism

Finding sustainable ways to change systems, processes, people, and organizations to lessen the magnitude of future crises

Some Examples

Coordinate relief efforts after a natural disaster

Join a committee that studies and makes recommendations for crisis management

Handle the emotional fallout from a disaster or crisis

Possible Lessons to Watch For

Connecting with those impacted in a language and tone that reflects how they are feeling brings some comfort

**Work outside
of your
home country
and culture**

Potential Features

Working in an unfamiliar culture or region

Learning a new language

Navigating new norms and rules

Some Examples

Do a stint at headquarters, in supply chain management, or in regional operations outside of your home country

Lead an expansion into new global markets

Manage outsourced operations

Adapt a marketing plan to a new global region

Sign up for a military, non-governmental organization (NGO), or State Department international deployment

Possible Lessons to Watch For

Adjusting your own behavior depending upon the cultural context and situation requires tremendous self-control and self-management

Take on a role that requires you to navigate complex, interpersonal issues

Potential Features

Dealing with complex people issues

Working with people who are different from you and from each other

Leading an inexperienced team

Leading a rapidly growing department or organization

Some Examples

Manage a team of recent graduates

Train and coordinate volunteers

Manage a dispersed, remote team

Lead a team through rapid growth or acquisition and integration

Possible Lessons to Watch For

The up-front investment you make in building relationships
pays dividends down the road

Influence without authority	**Potential Features**
	Pushing for changes and decisions that you do not have the authority to make
	Dealing with sensitive politics
	Managing people who have two bosses

Some Examples

Join an advisory board

Be a mentor

Mediate a conflict

Manage a matrixed team

Collaborate across boundaries on a critical, politically charged project

Possible Lessons to Watch For

Understanding and articulating disparate viewpoints helps you get your point of view across

Muster the courage to deal with poor performers

Potential Features

Downsizing a department

Making staff changes

Becoming known for recruiting and keeping "A" players

Some Examples

Be a mentor or a coach to a low performer

Deliver tough feedback

Make tough people decisions

Deliver a pink slip if necessary

Possible Lessons to Watch For

Being tough when necessary builds trust with high performers

Manage a team

Potential Features

Taking responsibility for the performance and development of a group of people

Providing direction and coaching to a team in order to accomplish a set of goals

Some Examples

Be a temporary manager—fill in for someone on leave

Manage a group process or project

Lead a team of your former peers

Lead a team where team members are experts but you aren't

Possible Lessons to Watch For

Getting things done through other people requires you to flex your style and approach

Expand your perspective

Potential Features

Having conversations with people who have different perspectives than you do

Reading about an unfamiliar topic

Some Examples

Take a vacation in a region or country you haven't visited before

Join a professional group

Negotiate a contract

Manage a dissatisfied customer and find a mutual resolution

Attend an executive development program

Possible Lessons to Watch For

Stepping outside your element can open up your mind and enable you to see things from an entirely different angle

Whether you seek out a special project or whether you see the chance to change careers, taking on experiences that place you squarely in interpersonally rich situations gives you the opportunity to practice people agile behaviors. These experiences might help you empathize with others, manage your reactions, and draw out people's best possible contributions. If you are motivated to continue building your own People Agility, here is what you can do:

Seek out experiences that challenge you to articulate different points of view, work through disagreements and conflict, and get things done through other people. Through these experiences, you will learn ways to stay open-minded, composed, and empathetic in a way that fosters better relationships.

Extract key lessons and principles that will inspire you to seek out and make amends with opponents, build partnerships, and inspire collective action that benefits everyone involved.

Use those insights in other situations as much as possible.

"Mediation is not about accepting the status quo and working with it. It is about reaching out to seemingly implacable foes and seeking to reassure that the interests of the conflict parties can be met, but through a transformation."

– Martti Ahtisaari

Learning Agility Factor

The extent to which
an individual likes change,
continuously explores new
options and solutions, and
is interested in leading
organizational change efforts

Change Agility
Agility
Promoting New Possibilities

Change Agility:
Promoting New Possibilities

Change agile people have the tendency to ask "what if?" and tinker with new ideas for the purpose of seeing continuous improvement. They move creative solutions from concept to adopted practice. And they are able to handle the heat and scrutiny that come with being cutting edge and leading change efforts.

Examples

Reveling in new ideas and possibilities

Challenging the status quo

Embracing risks

Testing and refining creative ideas

Seeking continuous improvement

Staying calm under pressure and uncertainty

Bringing others along by managing their resistance to change

Have you had the opportunity to observe and admire a masterful change agent in action? Someone who not only sees possibilities beyond what exists today, but can motivate others to adopt and champion the change? Change initiatives often fail, so it gives us pause when we witness leaders manage and sustain a transformation. How do they do it? Change agile people challenge the status quo by asking "what if?" They fiddle and tinker with new ideas until they land upon something that will make a difference. And they are a calm, steady presence through the course of emotions, scrutiny, resistance, and consequences that accompany change.

"We keep moving forward, opening new doors, and doing new things, because we're curious and curiosity keeps leading us down new paths."

– Walt Disney

Walt Disney is someone who dealt in imagination and possibility. Disney's ideas changed the field of entertainment in the 20th century. In every project, Disney pushed his "imagineers" to innovate in the areas of sound, character animation, storytelling, special effects, and specialized processes such as the multiplane camera. *Silly Symphonies,* a series of animated shorts, became the platform for Disney's experimentation with these methods. And while *Silly Symphonies* were

Walt Disney

a flop at the box office, the artistic and technological advances he made set the stage for Disney's later successes, including the breakthrough film *Snow White and the Seven Dwarves*—a harbinger of change for the industry. The *Snow White* project was controversial. As a full-length feature film, it was a departure from the animated short that was a formulaic success. The film industry dubbed the project "Disney's Folly," and even Disney's family members tried to talk him out of the project. But when the film premiered in 1937, the audience gave it a standing ovation. It went on to win an Oscar (along with seven miniature Oscars) and set the stage for the next 75 years of innovation and success in film for Walt Disney Studios.

It is common for change agile people to take risks and sometimes get it wrong at first. Experimenting, testing, and evaluating is a cycle that requires many attempts before zeroing in on the solution that will make a difference. Dedication to continuous improvement while staying composed through trial, failure, and criticism are trademarks of the change agile leader.

Florence Nightingale, the pioneer of modern nursing, risked her reputation by dedicating herself to improving medical care for the sick and wounded. At a time when the existence of germs was a theory and basic sanitation was experimental, Nightingale became convinced that sanitation was the most critical factor in reducing death rates in hospitals. Already taking the heat for being a working woman in the medical profession, Nightingale worked to convince other practitioners in her field that their current practices were ill-advised. She transformed the medical field by reducing fatalities in the civilian and military hospitals she worked in. Then she published her results in her book *Notes on Hospitals.* Her innovative visual presentation of statistics

Florence Nightingale

(she developed a new form of pie chart called the polar-area diagram) helped persuade others around the world that the changes she was making in hospital conditions were effective. Another book, *Notes on Nursing,* became a popular read not only for people in the budding nursing profession, but also for the general public. And in 1860, she founded the Nightingale Training School to train nurses and midwives. Ultimately, she led a transformation that established the foundation for modern nursing.

Florence Nightingale and Walt Disney took risks, experimented, made continuous improvements, and partnered with others to lead innovation in their fields. How does someone cultivate the attributes of a change agile leader? What formative experiences develop this ability? What wisdom gained and lessons learned shape a person's ability to identify innovative ideas and manage their successful adoption?

"No man, not even a doctor, ever gives any other definition of what a nurse should be than this: 'devoted and obedient.' This definition would do just as well for a porter. It might even do for a horse."

– Florence Nightingale

"If we are not achieving something,
it is because we have not put our
minds to it. We create what we want."

Muhammad Yunus – Bengali founder of Grameen Bank

Becoming Change Agile – Muhammad Yunus

Let's take a deeper look at an example that highlights the learning journey toward becoming change agile. Muhammad Yunus, the founder of the Grameen Bank and a pioneer of the microlending movement, found a way to provide credit to the poor. Traditional banks in Bangladesh required collateral, signatures, and a patriarch's permission before approving even the smallest loan. Exploitative local moneylenders filled the poor's unmet need for credit, but the steep interest rate and repayment terms only served to exacerbate the cycle of poverty. Yunus questioned the status quo, sought to remove hurdles, and found ways to improve the situation. Fueled by a belief that his actions could have a positive impact, Yunus was determined and persistent in pushing for change in the face of resistance.

Yunus' accomplishments were grounded in his studies in the field of economics, but there were many experiences that led him to be the provoking, ever-questioning conscience that sought ways to improve people's quality of life. Early experiences shaped the values, worldview, and personal qualities that led to his change agile behavior: His passion to ask challenging questions and to tirelessly experiment with solutions. Questions and experiments that would increase harvests during famine and provide capital to the world's poorest citizens.

How did Muhammad Yunus come to have the qualities that would put him at the forefront of such a significant economic movement? A look at some of his key experiences and the lessons he took from them provides insight into how he came to be compelled to change, mold, and effect change in the world.

> "My greatest challenge has been to change the mindset of people. Mindsets play strange tricks on us. We see things the way our minds have instructed our eyes to see."
>
> – Muhammad Yunus

Building
Change Agility

Muhammad Yunus' Experiences

1961–1965
Starts a packaging business
with a commercial loan

Just out of college, Yunus took a position teaching economics. He also kept himself busy with side projects. In the course of publishing a national literary magazine called *Uttaran* (Advancement), he discovered that there were no packaging or printing companies in East Pakistan. His father introduced him to someone who could help him get started in the business. Yunus applied for a loan, which was quickly approved, procured the machinery, and soon the plant produced products such as boxes, cartons, cards, calendars, and books. Within two years, the business made a modest profit and employed 100 people. It became clear to Yunus that he could succeed as an entrepreneur.

By moving ideas from concept to market, you can fill a need and make the venture profitable

Starting something new (like a magazine or a business) provides an opportunity to test out new ideas, products, and services

Access to start-up capital can create a sustainable business and income for many employees

These lessons develop the ability to take an idea from concept to market, test out new ideas, take financial risks, and create income for yourself and others.

Small Experiences – Big Lessons

Not all lessons come from monumental or arduous situations. Sometimes smaller-scale encounters bring profound and lasting insight. Many of Yunus' small experiences contributed to his foundational principles and worldview. Mainly, that he was an active participant in the world around him and he could effect change. Highlighted on these pages are a few experiences that contributed to his propensity to think in possibilities, test new ideas, and commit to improving the world around him.

1971
Leads a group of expatriates in support of Bangladeshi independence

As a Fulbright scholar at Vanderbilt University in the United States, Yunus received his Ph.D. in developmental economics, and later studied and taught in Tennessee. But in March 1971, a civil war broke out back home when Bangladesh declared independence from the Pakistani government. Yunus mobilized his fellow Bengalis (expats living in the U.S.), declared his allegiance to the independence movement, and made a motion to form and fund the Bangladesh Citizens' Committee on the spot. As secretary and spokesperson for the group, he worked to mobilize and coordinate Bengalis in the U.S., granted interviews that were nationally televised, and flew to Calcutta to help form a new Bangladesh government. Over the next several months, Yunus lobbied the U.S. House and Senate as well as foreign embassies, ran an information center, published *The Bangladesh Newsletter* from his apartment, and organized workshops on university campuses all over the U.S. By December 1971, after a devastating toll, Bangladesh won its war for independence.

Joining a revolution takes commitment and fortitude

Organizing and mobilizing like-minded people can impact the course of history

Persistent communication and appeal can garner support for your cause

These lessons build strength to endure the consequences and controversy that radical change engenders. These lessons also develop the savvy to organize people and resources in support of a change.

Pakistan's independence from India

By age 7, Yunus was already familiar with big political movements. His native Chittagong in Muslim Bengal became part of independent Pakistan in 1947. He remembers the exhilarating celebrations—speeches blaring, flags and banners flying, the streets crammed with people. He and his brother set off fireworks from their roof. At midnight on August 14, 1947, the electricity was switched off and a moment later when it was turned back on, a new country was born.

People can bring about change, and new nations can be born from their efforts

Translation to Change Agility:
Social and political movements can have real consequences.

1974
Seeks ways to end famine in
the village near his university

Boy Scouts

Yunus' Boy Scout troop leader became a mentor and moral influence who instilled in him a sense of responsibility to his community. Through fundraisers, trips, discussions, and rallies, Yunus was encouraged to aim high and channel his natural leadership ability for the betterment of his fellow human beings.

Being in relationship and community with others can be profoundly rewarding and can carry weighty responsibility

Translation to Change Agility:

Making a difference and seeking continuous improvement are rewarding pursuits.

As the head of the economics department at Chittagong University in Bangladesh, Yunus witnessed local villagers suffering from famine without any government intervention or support. He wrote a statement for the press, which was signed by the vice chancellor and other university faculty, declaring that the nation's leaders must mobilize to end the famine. On a local level, Yunus pursued possibilities for relief. The hills around the university could be converted to farmland, the rusty irrigation tubewells could be repaired and used by farmer co-ops, supplemental crops could be raised in the winter season, and high-yield rice could produce more food. Without a background in agriculture, Yunus set out partnering with local farmers and experimenting with new methods. The effort required full collaboration. Trust was built, knowledge was shared, risks were taken together. The attempt to transform farming methods was a joint mission with high stakes—the outcome could determine the fate of people's lives. The first year's harvest proved that their efforts were successful, but Yunus became aware of another pressing problem—the state of the landless poor.

Asking questions and partnering can introduce new perspectives and possibilities

In convincing others to explore new scenarios and take on risks, it helps to take on some of the risk yourself

These lessons reinforce the benefits that can come from asking "What if?" "Why?" "Why not?" and the power of a group working toward a common vision of the future.

1976
Meets Sufia who needs
twenty-two cents to
change her life

Somewhat bored by traditional teaching methods, Yunus ventured out of the classroom and into the local villages with his students, an approach he called "action research." In order to ground economic concepts in reality, Yunus sought out villagers to help him understand the state of their plight. A conversation with one young woman named Sufia made a lasting impression. She patiently answered his many questions while she continued to work on braiding the bamboo for the stools she made. Despite her work ethic, she was trapped in a short cycle of borrowing twenty-two cents for raw materials each morning, selling her products back to the lender in the evening, and clearing a two-cent profit every day. Yunus wanted to promote systemic change, not charity. But all of Sufia's suffering for a lack of twenty-two cents compelled him to make his first loan. Yunus' students surveyed the village and found that 42 women in the village were in a similar situation. A US$27 loan could free them from the crushing cycle of poverty. Yunus made this first loan from his own pocket, an act which spawned the Grameen Bank and the microlending movement.

As little as twenty-two cents could break the cycle of poverty for the world's poorest citizens

Ad hoc action is not enough; it needs to be institutionalized to make lasting change

These lessons reinforce the importance of questioning why something can't be done and then doing something about it.

Government bureaucracy
After Bangladesh won its independence, Yunus felt compelled to participate in nation-building. He took a job in the new government but quickly realized that the bureaucracy and passive indifference of government would not suit him. From what he saw, there was no sense of urgency or responsibility for rebuilding the devastated country. People were discouraged from proposing ideas because it would make their superiors look bad. Many used their positions for personal gain. After just two months, Yunus left his position, having developed a deep and enduring mistrust in government.

Without leadership, progress is stunted

Translation to Change Agility:
A passion for forward momentum will help you find ways to improve the lives of others.

"Why not?"

– Muhammad Yunus

Experiences
for building your
Change Agility

Yunus' Lessons Influenced His Approach to His Work

So many of Yunus' experiences encouraged and reinforced the change agile qualities that enabled him to embark on his most impactful change effort—the Grameen Bank and the microlending movement. Starting his own business taught him how identifying a need and having access to credit can build jobs. Experiencing the birth and rebirth of two nation states—first Pakistan and then Bangladesh—taught him that people can rally around a common vision and change the course of history. Witnessing inaction on the part of government and observing grassroots efforts of local farmers showed him how simple questions and ideas can become instituted practice and improve lives.

> "Well, I think the rules should be changed."
>
> – Muhammad Yunus

Yunus is a clear example of a change agile person. And he is a person shaped by his experiences. His orientation to future possibility was not empty optimism. He recognized the mountains he had to move and the difficulties involved. Conventional thinking, cultural norms, stubborn bankers, and political consequences were a few things he was up against, and yet he found ways to bring fresh ideas, tweak local practices, and collaborate with people to find better ways of growing food and lending money. His microcredit movement has empowered those he refers to as the "banking untouchables." The Grameen Bank provides a new source of credit so they can own their future. He pressed forward despite uncertainty and resistance, and he took personal risks that resulted in changing the lives of over 100 million of the world's poorest citizens.

Building Change Agility by Learning from Your Experiences

What inspiration do you draw from Yunus' journey toward becoming change agile? What connections can you make between his experiences and your own? Between past, present, and future, you may find that you have a strong starting point for discovering and developing your Change Agility. Both on-the-job and off-the-job experiences can have a powerful hand in developing your drive to get things done in new and challenging situations. As you begin to work on building more Change Agility, here are three reflection exercises to get you started.

Harvesting: Reaping Lessons from Past Experiences

Think about the significant experiences in your life that have developed your willingness to question the status quo, envision alternatives, and move forward with changes that might be controversial. What events, situations, hardships, or assignments stand out? When have you had the opportunity to test and refine creative ideas? Can you think of a situation that required you to convince others to go along with a change?

Exercise 1

Draw your own time line of key experiences that taught you about aspects of Change Agility, such as looking at things differently; experimenting with creative, new solutions; and making ideas a reality.

For each key experience on your time line, take a moment to describe what happened. Then describe what you took away from that experience.

What was the situation? What did you do and why?

What did you take away from that experience? Do those lessons have any earmarks of Change Agility?

How have you applied what you learned to other situations?

Learning in Real-Time: Extracting Lessons from Current Experiences

Think about current projects you are on, struggles you are experiencing, changes that you are going through in your life or career. How are these experiences exciting or how are they causing angst for you? Maybe you've identified a need and stepped in to make a difference, maybe trial and error hasn't produced a successful alternative yet, or maybe you are facing a backlash or negative response after implementing a controversial change.

Exercise 2

Describe two or three current experiences which are ripe for extracting lessons and principles about testing new ideas, making continuous improvements, getting changes adopted, or other aspects of Change Agility.

Make a note of what you are learning from each experience (here and now) to take with you into future situations.

What is the situation? How are you approaching it, and why are you taking that approach?

What lessons are beginning to emerge from this experience?

How might these lessons benefit you in the future?

Anticipating: Thoughtfully Planning for Future Experiences and Lessons

If you've decided that it would be to your advantage to build Change Agility, it's time to think ahead. You see how tinkering with the status quo and leading change will serve your personal and career goals. How do you go about building Change Agility? Do you wait for situations to happen or hardships to test your agility? Not necessarily. While some situations are out of your control (you can still learn from these), there are many valuable experiences you can proactively seek out.

Experiences that build Change Agility are situations that put you at the forefront of a change movement. Assignments that force you to question things, think in possibilities, work with others to bring ideas to fruition, and deal with real consequences of change. These experiences help develop a vision of an alternative future, the savvy to mobilize people, and the fortitude to withstand criticism and backlash. These are qualities of a change agile person.

Exercise 3

What is your goal? What is the result that you are looking for?
How will building Change Agility help you achieve your goal?
What does success look like?

Choose a few experiences that you would like to seek out in order to improve your Change Agility. These could be situations that are on the job or off the job, may be a part-time exploratory project, or a new full-time job that requires you to change departments, companies, or even relocate. Adjust the intensity-dial up or down depending on the size of the gap you are looking to close, the stage you're at in your career, and the level of challenge you are ready for.

Experiences to Sharpen Your Change Agility

Sponsor a high-visibility project

Potential Features

Handling formal negotiations with different groups, such as unions, governments, charities, or other bodies

Building visions, missions, charters, or strategies

Getting other people's ideas to come together under a tight deadline

Some Examples

Organize a fundraiser

Chair the board of an active nonprofit

Lead a strategic, groundbreaking project for your organization

Possible Lessons to Watch For

Thinking in possibilities can inspire a clearer picture of an alternative future

Lead a significant change effort

Potential Features

Introducing a change that could meet a lot of resistance

Getting buy-in and cooperation from others

Juggling multiple stakeholders and decision makers

Some Examples

Identify an unmet need and experiment with solutions that would fill the gap

Oversee the adoption of a new process or system

Lead a merger or acquisition

Possible Lessons to Watch For

Taking ideas and putting them into practice requires convincing and mobilizing teams and organizations

Turn around a business or product that is in a downward spiral

Potential Features

Going against the odds to deliver a tough project on time and on budget

Making tough decisions (trade-offs) that impact a variety of people

Taking charge and fixing something that is not working

Some Examples

Take on a tough project where your predecessor failed

Take over a line of business that is not breaking even and make it profitable

Relaunch an existing product or service that is not doing well

Possible Lessons to Watch For

Tight deadlines and getting one last chance to fix something can generate more creative and risky solutions because the threat of failure is imminent

Create a strategy and plan for an innovative service or product

Potential Features

Breaking new ground

Taking the heat from key stakeholders and decision makers

Shopping the strategy in order to have others challenge, adopt, and implement the ideas

Anticipating future scenarios

Some Examples

Do a rotation in a company strategy position

Commercialize a new product

Manage the expansion into new markets

Make a presentation to the board or executive leadership team

Possible Lessons to Watch For

By being forward-looking, you can find previously unexplored opportunities

Represent your group on an interdisciplinary project team

Potential Features

Cooperating with others

Meeting a tight deadline

Relying on others' expertise and contributions

Some Examples

Write a grant proposal

Sit on a task force

Form a joint venture or a strategic alliance

Possible Lessons to Watch For

Leading change in partnership with others is energizing

Take a job so complex that it makes your head spin

Potential Features

Dialing up the scope of your work and dealing with competing demands for your time

Increasing your visibility and responsibility

Taking on something that is outside your area of expertise

Handling complexity, uncertainty, and variety

Some Examples

Manage a department for the first time

Build e-commerce channel for outdated products/services

Integrate new products and services to an already full plate of offerings

Possible Lessons to Watch For

When you have many things going on at once, it forces you to take more risks

Take on a tough challenge	**Potential Features**
	Doing something that you dislike
	Handling the fallout from conflict or change
	Taking on projects that seem undoable

Some Examples

Mediate a difficult negotiation process

Shut something down

Manage a cost-cutting project

Serve a dissatisfied customer

Possible Lessons to Watch For

Maintaining your composure and staying calm under pressure is critical to making progress in difficult and uncertain conditions

Create or refine a complex system or process

Potential Features

Figuring out the best processes for getting things done

Getting others to adopt a new system or process

Some Examples

Launch a new system or process

Simplify a work process

Create contingency plans

Possible Lessons to Watch For

There are always opportunities to improve how work gets done

Whether you seek out an extracurricular project as a side dish to your current job or whether you see the chance to change careers, taking on experiences that press you to be at the forefront of change gives you the opportunity to try on change agile behaviors. These experiences might help you question traditions and assumptions, brainstorm alternatives, take action, and make a difference. If you are motivated to continue building your own Change Agility, here is what you can do:

Seek out experiences that challenge you to think differently, envision new possibilities, and transform your surroundings. Through these experiences, you will learn ways to handle the pressure, uncertainty, and controversy that accompany change.

Extract key lessons and principles that will inspire you to see new possibilities, test ideas, and work with others to bring lasting and sustainable change.

Use those insights in other situations as much as possible.

"It's kind of fun to do the impossible."

– Walt Disney

Learning Agility Factor

The degree to which
an individual is motivated by
challenge and can deliver results
in first-time and/or tough
situations through resourcefulness
and by inspiring others

Results

Agility

Making Things Happen

Results Agility:
Making Things Happen

Results agile people are motivated by challenge and can deliver results in new and tough situations. Their intense drive often inspires others to high achievement. With nimbleness, dexterity, and deftness, results agile people achieve results despite obstacles.

Examples

Getting things done under difficult, new, or ambiguous conditions

Motivating and inspiring others

Meeting obstacles with perseverance and resilience

Being adaptable and resourceful

Instilling confidence in others

> "Many of life's failures are people who did not realize how close they were to success when they gave up."
>
> – Thomas Edison

Have you ever marveled at how resilient some people can be in the face of hardship? Despite a cut in funding, a canceled project, sabotage, or worse, these people tend to bounce back with a new approach. Like water, they find ways to get around, under, or through.

Take Thomas Edison, for example. He had enough failed experiments to fill the Library of Congress. Rather than getting discouraged by his failed attempts to develop a storage battery, he's quoted as saying, "I have not failed. I've just found 10,000 ways that won't work." He chose to use his failed experiments as insights to be applied to the next experiment. At the end of his career, Edison held over a thousand patents for his inventions.

Results agile people seem to have an endless fountain of energy which attracts a followership. With their resilience, perseverance, work ethic, and earnestness, you find yourself first rooting for them, then joining them and working toward the same goal. There is an inspiring, contagious quality—in part because the confidence they have in themselves instills confidence in others. If they have a competitive spirit, it is them against the forces that would prevent them from achieving what they set out to do. With this gale force—they build and inspire teams to make things happen in uncharted territory.

Thomas Edison

Amelia Earhart dabbled in various professional interests before she turned her attention to flying. On a visit to a California airfield, a ride in an airplane solidified her ambition: "By the time I had got two or three hundred feet off the ground, I knew I had to fly." She became the sixteenth American woman to be issued a pilot's license. Even after a few harrowing flights, Earhart emerged motivated to improve her skills and eager to take on the next challenge. She took up competitive flying and within five years set seven women's speed and distance aviation records. In 1932, at the age of 34, Earhart became the first woman to fly solo nonstop across the Atlantic. In 1935, she became the first person to fly solo from Hawaii to California. Her career, her celebrity endorsements, her promotion of commercial air travel, and her establishment of the Ninety-Nines, an organization to support women in aviation, made her an inspirational figure for a generation of female aviators. Earhart's drive and accomplishments continue to motivate career-minded, goal-oriented pioneers in many fields.

Amelia Earhart

Thomas Edison and Amelia Earhart clearly demonstrated a tireless perseverance and the ability to get results in challenging circumstances. But how does a person acquire those attributes? You may have a particular disposition, genetic makeup, personality, or set of early life experiences, but none of these would exclude you from being hardworking, resilient, and perseverant. There is an element of choice. What experiences do you choose? What do you choose to take away from those experiences? And what do you do with those lessons learned?

"Never do things others can do and will do, if there are things others cannot do or will not do."

– Amelia Earhart

"You cannot keep determined people from success.
If you place stumbling blocks in their way,
they will use them for stepping-stones
and climb to new heights."

Mary Kay Ash – American entrepreneur

Becoming Results Agile – Mary Kay Ash

Let's take a deeper look at another example that highlights the learning journey toward becoming results agile. Mary Kay Ash, the founder of Mary Kay Inc., maintained tremendous drive and fortitude despite her circumstances. When you read about her life and business, there are many points at which you might assume she would have yielded to the pressure and quit. But she kept on going. She was tenacious and not inclined to capitulate.

Ash is a textbook case of Results Agility. When confronted with an obstacle or impediment, she put her shoulder into it and moved ahead with a fierce determination. Ash was doggedly optimistic about what she and others could accomplish. The infectious nature of her resilient spirit inspired others to find those qualities in themselves and rally in support of achieving something great together.

But how did Ash come to have these qualities? A look at some of her key experiences and the lessons she took from them provide a window into how she became so driven and resourceful.

"Aerodynamically, the bumblebee shouldn't be able to fly, but the bumblebee doesn't know it so it goes on flying anyway."

– Mary Kay Ash

Building
Results Agility

Mary Kay Ash's Experiences

1920s
Takes care of sick father while
mother works 14-hour shifts

In her formative years, Ash took care of her ailing father while her mother worked 14-hour shifts to provide for their family. Despite the material disadvantages, her mother continued to provide emotional encouragement and fortitude to Ash. The mantra "you can do it" was a familiar one. Ash was taking to heart the lessons that would shape her approach to life's future challenges.

Small Experiences – Big Lessons

Not all lessons come from monumental or arduous situations. Sometimes a brief encounter brings lasting insight. Many of the business principles that carried Ash to achieve results in her career were things she learned from brief encounters. Highlighted on these pages are a few that contributed to her ability to be nimble, resourceful, and steadfast in her endeavors.

Work hard and persevere

You can do it

You have people supporting you and counting on you

These lessons build a strong personal drive and the ability to pull things off under difficult conditions.

1940s
Finds herself in survival
mode: a divorced, single mom
with three small children

After returning home from World War II, Ash's husband asked for a divorce. With her confidence and identity shaken, Ash found herself with three young children to support. She felt like a failure. Her emotional state wreaked havoc on her body, leading doctors to diagnose her with rheumatoid arthritis. As a matter of survival, Ash took up a new career in direct selling. She realized quickly that sales suffered when people saw her struggle or make excuses. Stakes were high. Without sales, she would not be able to put food on her table. She quickly learned to do her best and demonstrate confidence, no matter how she felt that day. Many of the lessons from this experience helped her build a successful career.

It pays to be self-confident

Leave personal problems at home

Always present your best self

Act enthusiastic and you will become enthusiastic

These lessons instill confidence and foster a never-give-up attitude.

Skin care class
After hosting her first skin care class, Ash was mortified because she had only sold $1.50 worth of product. In her embarrassment, she went over the sales demonstration in her mind. After succumbing to her initial temptation to blame others and doubt herself, she realized that her fear of failure had prevented her from asking for people's orders. She didn't even pass out order forms or her business cards.

Ask for the sale

Translation to Results Agility:
Confidence and commitment are critical to get the desired result.

Before the pink Cadillac

With cash in her pocket, Ash set off to buy a two-toned Ford as a birthday present to herself. She was dismissed by the salesman who did not take her seriously or treat her with much respect. After being ignored, she crossed the street to look at the Mercury dealer's showroom. A courteous salesman made her feel like a valued and legitimate customer. He even brought out a bouquet of flowers when he found out it was her birthday. He made her feel important. She bought a yellow Mercury.

Make people feel important

Translation to Results Agility:
Motivating others enables you to get things done through others.

1950s
Builds a career in sales and training, working against gender bias

Ash ascended in her sales career and eventually began to train other members of the sales team. Well-positioned for a promotion, she found herself passed over again and again by the men she trained. She took note of the gender discrimination she faced: less pay for equal work, overlooked for promotions, condescending attitudes from her male counterparts. The insights she gleaned from the situation gave her a desire to take her success into her own hands.

When you can't change the environment around you, create a new environment

You need to create your own opportunities

Thinking like a woman isn't a bad thing—sales tactics that incorporate soft skills (stereotypically associated with women) often lead to better sales

These lessons build a strong drive to succeed, despite obstacles.

1963

Rejects retirement and invests personal savings to start Mary Kay Inc.

A pivotal year for Mary Kay Ash. She retired from a successful sales and training career. But she realized that retirement would not suit her. Her reflections on the fundamental ingredients required to build a dream company for women had turned into a business plan (and later a book articulating her signature leadership principles). Ash had remarried, and with her husband as the head of finance and Ash as the head of sales and marketing, she was ready to launch Mary Kay Inc. Sadly, Ash's husband died suddenly, one month before Mary Kay® opened. Ash considered giving up her dream. Instead, she tapped into her tenacious spirit, and with the support of family, she opened the doors of Beauty by Mary Kay® on September 13, 1963, as planned.

Passion for what you believe in (a business for and by women) is not something you can put on the shelf in retirement

When a critical partner is taken from you, other people and resources are available to you

Never rest on your laurels—as long as you're living, continue to work hard to achieve your goals

These lessons build resilience and adaptability when faced with changing circumstances.

Marriage advice

A colleague sought out Ash for advice on her marriage. Without knowing the husband or the situation, Ash chose to listen and ask questions rather than weigh in with advice. Before long, her colleague had come to some resolution about the best course of action. All Ash had done was listen and inquire—an approach she successfully applied later with customers and sales consultants.

Listen long enough and people will arrive at a plan of action

Translation to Results Agility:
Empowering others can mobilize people to take action and get results.

"For every failure,
there's an alternative course of action.
You just have to find it.
When you come to a roadblock,
take a detour."

– Mary Kay Ash

Experiences
for building your
Results Agility

Ash's Lessons Influenced Her Approach to Her Work

It seems clear that the lessons Ash drew from her experiences fueled her ability to get results in later situations. Lessons learned from starting up a company enabled her to start the Mary Kay Foundation℠, dedicated to combating domestic violence against women and searching for cures for cancers that affect women. Learning that she could seize opportunities, find resources, and build a business based on her beliefs and principles were lessons Ash applied when she took the company from publicly held to privately held in 1983. Her lesson to never rest on her laurels informed how the company rewarded Independent Beauty Consultants and fueled the company's consistent growth.

> "Never rest on your laurels. Nothing wilts faster than a laurel sat upon."
>
> – Mary Kay Ash

In providing an overview of Ash's key experiences and results, the intent is not to make you a Mary Kay Ash expert, but to illustrate how learning from experiences can shape Results Agility. Ash was not born a results agile businesswoman. Her collected experiences and hardships provided her with opportunities to build her Results Agility. Ash's willingness to learn from these experiences enabled her to carry lessons and principles into each next venture. The culmination of which was a business that started with a $5,000 personal investment and has grown to over $3 billion in annual sales.

Building Results Agility by Learning from Your Experiences

What connections can you make between Ash's experiences and your own? What inspiration do you draw from her journey toward becoming results agile? Between past, present, and future, you may find that you have a strong starting point for discovering and developing your Results Agility. Both on-the-job and off-the-job experiences can have a powerful hand in developing your drive to get things done in new and challenging situations. As you begin to work on building more Results Agility, here are three reflection exercises to get you started.

Harvesting: Reaping Lessons from Past Experiences

Think about the significant experiences in your life that have called upon you to get things done through other people, be resourceful, deliver results under difficult conditions, and persevere. What events, situations, hardships, or assignments stand out? When have you had to get something done in a short time frame with very few resources? Can you recollect a time when you were challenged to do something beyond what you thought you could do?

Exercise 1

Draw your own time line of key experiences that taught you about aspects of Results Agility, such as perseverance, resourcefulness, and adaptability in difficult, new, or ambiguous situations.

For each key experience on your time line, take a moment to describe what happened. Then describe what you took away from that experience.

What was the situation? What did you do and why?

What did you take away from that experience? Do those lessons have any of the earmarks of Results Agility?

How have you applied what you learned to other situations?

Learning in Real-Time: Extracting Lessons from Current Experiences

Think about current projects you are on, struggles you are experiencing, changes that you are going through in your life or career. How are these experiences exciting or how are they causing angst for you? Maybe you are leading a new project for a breakthrough product, maybe you are banging your head against the wall trying to turn around a failing business, or perhaps you are working toward a shared goal as part of a neighborhood committee.

Exercise 2

Describe two or three current experiences which are ripe for extracting lessons and principles about getting results despite challenging circumstances or other qualities of Results Agility.

Make a note of what you are learning from each experience (here and now) to take with you into future situations.

What is the situation? How are you approaching it, and why are you taking that approach?

What lessons are beginning to emerge from this experience?

How might these lessons benefit you in the future?

Anticipating: Thoughtfully Planning for Future Experiences and Lessons

If you've decided that it would be to your advantage to build Results Agility, it's time to look ahead. You see how resourcefulness, a drive to achieve, and the ability to motivate and inspire others to rally around the same goal will serve your personal and career goals. How do you go about building Results Agility? Do you wait for situations to happen or hardships to test your agility? Not necessarily. While you can learn many lessons from situations that are out of your control, there are many valuable experiences you can proactively seek out.

Experiences that build Results Agility are usually high-stakes assignments where it will be clear whether you succeed or fail. Assignments that force you to go for gold in unfamiliar circumstances—maybe with a new team, a new company, a new product, a different go-to-market strategy. Changing it up adds a challenge that will create the need to be resourceful, agile, to rely on others, to call upon your personal drive, and to persevere. These are the qualities of a results agile person.

Exercise 3

What is your goal? What is the result that you are looking for? How will building Results Agility help you achieve your goal? What does success look like?

Choose a few experiences that you would like to seek out in order to improve your Results Agility. These could be situations that are on the job or off the job, may be a part-time extracurricular assignment (like the 20% Google allows employees for special, exploratory projects), or a new full-time job that requires you to change departments, companies, or even relocate. Adjust the intensity-dial up or down depending on the size of the gap you are looking to close, the stage you're at in your career, and the level of challenge you are ready for.

Experiences to Sharpen Your Results Agility

Lead a significant change effort

Potential Features

Introducing a change that could meet a lot of resistance

Getting buy-in and cooperation from others

Juggling multiple stakeholders and decision makers

Some Examples

Convince the office to outsource a service (e.g., printing, recruiting, call center)

Restructure a business

Transform a product line to accommodate changing customer needs

Possible Lessons to Watch For

Letting natural consequences take their course helps you avoid being the bad guy

Solve a crisis for people

Potential Features

Leading others during an unpredictable and scary time

Being a spokesperson to the company and the public; enduring intense scrutiny and criticism

Finding sustainable ways to change systems, processes, people, and organizations to lessen the magnitude of future crises

Some Examples

Solve urgent key supplier or vendor problems

Manage a global safety recall of a major brand

Deal with product-tampering threats or shut down a plant

Possible Lessons to Watch For

Resources can be found in unlikely places. When directed, people will rally to help

Turn around a business or product that is in a downward spiral

Potential Features

Risking failure but trying to deliver a tough project on time and on budget anyway

Making tough decisions (trade-offs) that impact a variety of people

Some Examples

Become a spokesperson for a struggling business or product line

Lead a business out of bankruptcy

Fix a lemon

Revive a tarnished brand

Possible Lessons to Watch For

The first and second failed attempts can sometimes lead to a third option that had not been considered before

Find a job that takes what you do well and then super-sizes it

Potential Features

Taking responsibility for something beyond what you think you can do

Taking on a bigger region, a bigger budget, or a higher number of locations

Some Examples

Move from store manager to district manager

Head up your function for entire enterprise

Possible Lessons to Watch For

You can shoulder more responsibility by delegating appropriately and getting results through other people

Run your own business

Potential Features

Building a high-performing team from scratch

Taking over something that is off to a fast start

Some Examples

Be an independent consultant

Run a side business related to a hobby or personal interest

Be an entrepreneur

Possible Lessons to Watch For

Being responsible for both business strategy and operations builds the confidence and resilience necessary to handle obstacles and changing circumstances that inevitably arise

Build something from scratch

Potential Features

Running a start-up

Taking something already started and reworking it nearly from scratch

Some Examples

Be employee number one or two for a growing business

Launch a new brand or product

Get seed funding from the board for a new project

Set up a new office in a new location

Possible Lessons to Watch For

When you tap into what really excites you about your work,
it ceases to be work

Take on a tough challenge	**Potential Features**
	Doing something that you dislike
	Handling the fallout from conflict or change
	Taking on projects that seem undoable

Some Examples

Take over a failing project

Lead an under-resourced project

Work for a talented but difficult boss

Agree to do a task that you dislike

Motivate other people to accomplish something very difficult

Possible Lessons to Watch For

Taking on a challenge builds confidence; it makes you realize that you are stronger than you thought

Manage a team

Potential Features

Taking responsibility for the performance and development of a group of people

Providing direction and coaching to a team in order to accomplish a set of goals

Some Examples

Turn around a team of low performers that you inherited

Manage a group of people outside of your area of expertise

Lead an inexperienced team

Possible Lessons to Watch For

You can motivate and instill confidence in a team to the point that all are amazed by what can be accomplished

Big and small experiences have the potential to provide "aha" moments that build the perseverance, adaptability, resilience, and drive that are ever present in results agile people. If you are motivated to continue building your own Results Agility, here is what you can do:

Seek out experiences that challenge you to move ahead in the face of obstacles and to get results no matter the situation.

Extract key lessons and principles that will help you achieve results and persevere.

Use those insights in other situations as much as possible.

"The most difficult thing is the decision to act,
the rest is merely tenacity.
The fears are paper tigers.
You can do anything you decide to do."

– Amelia Earhart

Afterword

The pages of this book are filled with examples of exceptional leaders who seized their life experiences (both planned and unplanned) to cultivate their Learning Agility.

Self-Awareness

When Maya Angelou listened and heeded feedback from a vocal coach, she was building awareness of her strengths and weaknesses.

Mental Agility

When Albert Einstein reviewed "uncommonly diversified" patent applications with skepticism and an inquiring mind, he was exercising his curiosity, making fresh connections, and broadening his perspective.

People Agility

When Nelson Mandela witnessed his village chief hear grievances and reach consensus, he was learning how to listen and understand different points of view.

Change Agility

When Muhammad Yunus led
fellow expatriates in support of the
Bangladeshi independence movement,
he was learning how to organize
resources and people in support
of social and political change.

Results Agility

When Mary Kay Ash hosted her
first skin care class and only made
a $1.50 sale, she was learning what
it takes to get results.

These social, political, and business leaders have made a lasting impact on our world. Reflecting on the course of their lives reveals how they were shaped by their experiences and the lessons they drew from those experiences.

Knowing that becoming an agile leader is built upon the intersection of your experiences and the ability to learn from those experiences, what new experiences will you seek out? How will you extract as much meaning as possible from those experiences? How will you apply those lessons and principles to future challenges?

How will you intentionally and mindfully practice learning from your experiences? Consider using the suggested process highlighted in the introduction:

Experience – Seek out a challenging experience and immerse yourself in it...

What will push you beyond
what you already know how to do?

What difficult task seems undoable?

Where are there significant obstacles
that need to be overcome?

Observe – Stay mindful as you notice how the situation unfolds...

What history or background information
could be helpful?

Who are the players involved?

What is the desired outcome?

Reflect – Take the time to make sense of the experience...

Why did you choose to approach
the situation the way you did?

What felt most challenging? Why?

What did you find surprising? Why?

Distill – Extract insight, wisdom, rules of thumb, or guiding principles from the experience...

What would you do differently next time?

What meaning do you attribute to the experience?

How would you coach someone going through
a similar experience?

Apply – Find ways to use those lessons in other situations...

What lessons equip you for taking on bigger challenges?

How do the lessons you learned reframe how
you think about or approach new experiences?

What are some underlying similarities
in the new situations you encounter?

As Charles Darwin observed, "It is not the strongest of the species that survives, nor the most intelligent, but the one most responsive to change." Adaptability—responsiveness and adjustment to new conditions or situations—requires the ability to learn from experiences, apply those lessons, and make changes. Your ability to function and prosper both personally and professionally depends upon your ability to learn and adapt. How can you ensure that you are continuously learning and adapting?

Practice taking on a learner's mind-set. Find a learner's mantra that works for you. Something like, *"The only real failure in life is the failure to try."* Be curious and inquisitive. Find new interests both at work and outside of work. Read up on a variety of topics. Relish ambiguity. Work at solving new problems with approaches you've never tried before. Question the status quo. Be creative in finding new resources. Remember not to get too hung up on the outcome of the experience. Lessons can be learned just as deeply when things go wrong as when things go right. These approaches and mind-sets will assist you in becoming a more agile leader.

Like many pursuits, becoming an agile leader can be a lifelong endeavor. But that doesn't mean it will take you decades to see changes and improvements to your learning agility. Lessons and insights you glean from your experiences can benefit you every day—including today.

Exercises: Learning from Your Experiences

Building Your
Self-Awareness

Reaping Lessons from Past Experiences

Think about significant experiences in your life that have caused you to reflect, take stock, and arrive at a higher level of self-understanding. What events, situations, hardships, or assignments stand out? In which experiences did you learn the most about yourself? Which ones showcased your strengths? Or uncovered weaknesses you weren't previously aware of? When did seeking feedback from others help you learn about yourself? And what did you do with that increased self-understanding?

Exercise 1: Harvesting

Draw your own time line of key experiences that caused you to pause and do some self-reflection. These may have been instances where you received surprising feedback, made a mistake, or learned something new.

For each key experience on your time line, take a moment to describe what happened. Then describe what you took away from that experience.

What was the situation? What did you do and why?

What did you take away from that experience? Do those lessons have any earmarks of Self-Awareness?

How have you applied what you learned to other situations?

Use the space provided to make notes.

Building Your
Self-Awareness

Extracting Lessons
from Current Experiences

Think about current projects you are on, struggles you are experiencing, changes that you are going through in your life or career. How are these experiences exciting or how are they causing angst for you? Perhaps you are struggling with some strong feelings, maybe you need clarity before making a decision, or maybe you've received some constructive feedback that was difficult to hear and has given you pause.

Exercise 2: Learning in Real-Time

Describe two or three current experiences which are ripe for extracting lessons and principles about self-reflection, seeking feedback, or being honest with yourself and others about your strengths and weaknesses.

Make a note of what you are learning from each experience (here and now) to take with you into future situations.

What is the situation? How are you approaching it, and why are you taking that approach?

What lessons are beginning to emerge from this experience?

How might these lessons benefit you in the future?

Use the space provided to make notes.

Building Your
Self-Awareness
Thoughtfully Planning for
Future Experiences and Lessons

Experiences that build Self-Awareness are situations that are challenging—whether it's because they are emotionally laden; require new skills; have complex, interpersonal dynamics; or highlight some dissonance between your beliefs and your actions. Assignments that, in order to succeed, force you to be honest with yourself and candid with others about your shortcomings. These experiences help develop the ability to reflect and gain a clearer understanding of what you're good at and not so good at. And if the not so good is standing between you and your goals, doing something about it. These are actions of a self-aware leader.

Exercise 3: Anticipating

Choose a few experiences that you would like to seek out in order to improve your Self-Awareness.

What is your goal? What is the result that you are looking for?

How will building Self-Awareness help you achieve your goal?

What does success look like?

Use the space provided to make notes.

EXPERIENCES

Risk everything and take on a new role

Work outside of your home country and culture

Start something new and unique for you, your company, or customers

Take a job so complex that it makes your head spin

Move to the field if you're at corporate (or vice versa)

Learn something new

Get involved outside of work

Teach others

Building Your
Mental Agility

Reaping Lessons from Past Experiences

Think about the significant experiences in your life that have inspired you to be curious, bring a fresh perspective to a complex problem, or help others think things through. What events, situations, hardships, or assignments stand out? In what circumstance did you have that "aha" moment where everything came into focus and the solution to a tough problem presented itself? When did being curious lead you to discover new ways of viewing things?

Exercise 1: Harvesting

Draw your own time line of key experiences that taught you about aspects of Mental Agility, such as integrating different perspectives, analyzing a complex problem, or getting to the root cause of an issue.

For each key experience on your time line, take a moment to describe what happened. Then describe what you took away from that experience.

What was the situation? What did you do and why?

What did you take away from that experience? Do those lessons have any earmarks of Mental Agility?

How have you applied what you learned to other situations?

Use the space provided to make notes.

Building Your
Mental Agility
Extracting Lessons
from Current Experiences

Think about current projects you are on, struggles you are experiencing, changes that you are going through in your life or career. How are these experiences exciting or how are they causing angst for you? Maybe you are sifting through a complex problem trying to find the nuggets of meaning, maybe you are on the verge of an inspired idea that marries the best of two worlds, or maybe you found yourself wondering why and you are indulging your curiosity.

Exercise 2: Learning in Real-Time

Describe two or three current experiences which are ripe for extracting lessons and principles about aspects of Mental Agility, such as curiosity, analytical thinking, and looking at things differently.

Make a note of what you are learning from each experience (here and now) to take with you into future situations.

What is the situation? How are you approaching it, and why are you taking that approach?

What lessons are beginning to emerge from this experience?

How might these lessons benefit you in the future?

Use the space provided to make notes.

Building Your
Mental Agility
Thoughtfully Planning for
Future Experiences and Lessons

Experiences that build Mental Agility are situations that challenge your assumptions, expand your perspective, and increase the cognitive load you can carry. Assignments that force you to analyze or evaluate a strategic approach, solve a conundrum, generate viable alternatives to the status quo, or figure out something when you don't have all the information. These experiences help develop cognitive flexibility, tolerance for ambiguity, the ability to embrace complexity, and the clarity of thought to articulate ideas elegantly. These are the qualities of a mentally agile person.

Exercise 3: Anticipating

Choose a few experiences that you would like to seek out in order to improve your Mental Agility.

What is your goal? What is the result that you are looking for?

How will building Mental Agility help you achieve your goal?

What does success look like?

Use the space provided to make notes.

EXPERIENCES

Lead a project team

Take responsibility for delivering a viable business strategy

Start something new and unique for you, your company, or customers

Risk everything and take on a new role

Turn around a business or product that is in a downward spiral

Take a job so complex that it makes your head spin

Take on an individual project

Expand your perspective

Building Your
People Agility

Reaping Lessons from Past Experiences

Think about the significant experiences in your life that challenged you to relate to people. Maybe the situation required you to relate to your audience; have a calm demeanor in a tense, interpersonal situation; understand someone else's perspective; or to give credit and let others shine. What events, situations, hardships, or assignments stand out? What situations have led you to empathize with others? What circumstances have required you to keep an open mind to alternative points of view?

Exercise 1: Harvesting

Draw your own time line of key experiences that taught you about aspects of People Agility, such as building rapport, relating to people who see the world very differently from you, and constructively managing conflict.

For each key experience on your time line, take a moment to describe what happened. Then describe what you took away from that experience.

What was the situation? What did you do and why?

What did you take away from that experience? Do those lessons have any earmarks of People Agility?

How have you applied what you learned to other situations?

Use the space provided to make notes.

Building Your
People Agility

Extracting Lessons
from Current Experiences

Think about current projects you are on, struggles you are experiencing, changes that you are going through in your life or career. How are these experiences exciting or how are they causing angst for you? Perhaps you are struggling to stay composed and objective in an interpersonal conflict, maybe you see the opportunity to be more open-minded and flexible, or maybe you see the opportunity to cultivate relationships with others.

Exercise 2: Learning in Real-Time

Describe two or three current experiences which are ripe for extracting lessons and principles about aspects of People Agility, such as reading people, adjusting your approach, defusing tension, and getting the best out of people.

Make a note of what you are learning from each experience (here and now) to take with you into future situations.

What is the situation? How are you approaching it, and why are you taking that approach?

What lessons are beginning to emerge from this experience?

How might these lessons benefit you in the future?

Use the space provided to make notes.

Building Your
People Agility

Thoughtfully Planning for
Future Experiences and Lessons

Experiences that build People Agility are situations that demand seeing things from diverse points of view, navigating emotions and politics, and managing your reactions even when you feel strongly. Assignments that force you to deal with uncomfortable situations, reach consensus with opposing groups, and communicate with people in a way that speaks to them on many levels. These experiences help develop the interpersonal warmth and calm that can build bridges, with the potential to influence productive, collective efforts. These are qualities of a people agile leader.

Exercise 3: Anticipating

Choose a few experiences that you would like to seek out in order to improve your People Agility.

What is your goal? What is the result that you are looking for?

How will building People Agility help you achieve your goal?

What does success look like?

Use the space provided to make notes.

EXPERIENCES

Lead a significant change effort

Solve a crisis for people

Work outside of your home country and culture

Take on a role that requires you to navigate complex, interpersonal issues

Influence without authority

Muster the courage to deal with poor performers

Manage a team

Expand your perspective

Building Your
Change Agility
Reaping Lessons from Past Experiences

Think about the significant experiences in your life that have developed your willingness to question the status quo, envision alternatives, and move forward with changes that might be controversial. What events, situations, hardships, or assignments stand out? When have you had the opportunity to test and refine creative ideas? Can you think of a situation that required you to convince others to go along with a change?

Exercise 1: Harvesting

Draw your own time line of key experiences that taught you about aspects of Change Agility, such as looking at things differently; experimenting with creative, new solutions; and making ideas a reality.

For each key experience on your time line, take a moment to describe what happened. Then describe what you took away from that experience.

What was the situation? What did you do and why?

What did you take away from that experience? Do those lessons have any earmarks of Change Agility?

How have you applied what you learned to other situations?

Use the space provided to make notes.

Building Your
Change Agility

Extracting Lessons
from Current Experiences

Think about current projects you are on, struggles you are experiencing, changes that you are going through in your life or career. How are these experiences exciting or how are they causing angst for you? Maybe you've identified a need and stepped in to make a difference, maybe trial and error hasn't produced a successful alternative yet, or maybe you are facing a backlash or negative response after implementing a controversial change.

Exercise 2: Learning in Real-Time

Describe two or three current experiences which are ripe for extracting lessons and principles about testing new ideas, making continuous improvements, getting changes adopted, or other aspects of Change Agility.

Make a note of what you are learning from each experience (here and now) to take with you into future situations.

What is the situation? How are you approaching it, and why are you taking that approach?

What lessons are beginning to emerge from this experience?

How might these lessons benefit you in the future?

Use the space provided to make notes.

Building Your
Change Agility

Thoughtfully Planning for
Future Experiences and Lessons

Experiences that build Change Agility are situations that put you at the forefront of a change movement. Assignments that force you to question things, think in possibilities, work with others to bring ideas to fruition, and deal with real consequences of change. These experiences help develop a vision of an alternative future, the savvy to mobilize people, and the fortitude to withstand criticism and backlash. These are qualities of a change agile person.

Exercise 3: Anticipating

Choose a few experiences that you would like to seek out in order to improve your Change Agility.

What is your goal? What is the result that you are looking for?

How will building Change Agility help you achieve your goal?

What does success look like?

Use the space provided to make notes.

EXPERIENCES

Sponsor a high-visibility project

Lead a significant change effort

Turn around a business or product that is in a downward spiral

Create a strategy and plan for an innovative service or product

Represent your group on an interdisciplinary project team

Take a job so complex that it makes your head spin

Take on a tough challenge

Create or refine a complex system or process

Building Your
Results Agility

Reaping Lessons from Past Experiences

Think about the significant experiences in your life that have called upon you to get things done through other people, be resourceful, deliver results under difficult conditions, and persevere. What events, situations, hardships, or assignments stand out? When have you had to get something done in a short time frame with very few resources? Can you recollect a time when you were challenged to do something beyond what you thought you could do?

Exercise 1: Harvesting

Draw your own time line of key experiences that taught you about aspects of Results Agility, such as perseverance, resourcefulness, and adaptability in difficult, new, or ambiguous situations.

For each key experience on your time line, take a moment to describe what happened. Then describe what you took away from that experience.

What was the situation? What did you do and why?

What did you take away from that experience? Do those lessons have any of the earmarks of Results Agility?

How have you applied what you learned to other situations?

Use the space provided to make notes.

Building Your
Results Agility

Extracting Lessons
from Current Experiences

Think about current projects you are on, struggles you are experiencing, changes that you are going through in your life or career. How are these experiences exciting or how are they causing angst for you? Maybe you are leading a new project for a breakthrough product, maybe you are banging your head against the wall trying to turn around a failing business, or perhaps you are working toward a shared goal as part of a neighborhood committee.

Exercise 2: Learning in Real-Time

Describe two or three current experiences which are ripe for extracting lessons and principles about getting results despite challenging circumstances or other qualities of Results Agility.

Make a note of what you are learning from each experience (here and now) to take with you into future situations.

What is the situation? How are you approaching it, and why are you taking that approach?

What lessons are beginning to emerge from this experience?

How might these lessons benefit you in the future?

Use the space provided to make notes.

Building Your
Results Agility

Thoughtfully Planning for
Future Experiences and Lessons

Experiences that build Results Agility are usually high-stakes assignments where it will be clear whether you succeed or fail. Assignments that force you to go for gold in unfamiliar circumstances—maybe with a new team, a new company, a new product, a different go-to-market strategy. Changing it up adds a challenge that will create the need to be resourceful, agile, to rely on others, to call upon your personal drive, and to persevere. These are the qualities of a results agile person.

Exercise 3: Anticipating

Choose a few experiences that you would like to seek out in order to improve your Results Agility.

What is your goal? What is the result that you are looking for?

How will building Results Agility help you achieve your goal?

What does success look like?

Use the space provided to make notes.

EXPERIENCES

Lead a significant change effort

Solve a crisis for people

Turn around a business or product that is in a downward spiral

Find a job that takes what you do well and then super-sizes it

Run your own business

Build something from scratch

Take on a tough challenge

Manage a team

Notes

1. George, B. (with Sims, P.). (2007). *True north: Discover your authentic leadership.* San Francisco, CA: Jossey-Bass.

2. McCall, M. W., Jr., Lombardo, M. M., & Morrison, A. M. (1988). *The lessons of experience: How successful executives develop on the job.* New York, NY: The Free Press.

3. Lombardo, M. M., & Eichinger, R. W. (2011). *The leadership machine: Architecture to develop leaders for any future* (10th Anniversary ed.). Minneapolis, MN: Lominger International: A Korn/Ferry Company.

4. McCall, M. W., Jr., & Hollenbeck, G. P. (2002). *Developing global executives: The lessons of international experience.* Boston, MA: Harvard Business School Press.

5. Yip, J., & Wilson, M. (2008). *Developing public service leaders in Singapore* [Research Overview]. Singapore: Center for Creative Leadership.

6. Zhang, Y., Chandrasekar, N., & Wei, R. (2009). *Developing Chinese leaders in the 21st century* [Research Overview]. Singapore: Center for Creative Leadership and Shanghai, China: Europe International Business School.

7. Wilson, M. (2008). *Developing future leaders for high-growth Indian companies: New perspectives* [Research Overview]. Singapore: Center for Creative Leadership and Pune, India: Tata Management Training Center.

8. Lombardo, M. M., & Eichinger, R. W. (2000). High potentials as high learners. *Human Resource Management, 39*(4), 321–330.

9. Lombardo, M. M., & Eichinger, R. W. (1989). *Eighty-eight assignments for development in place.* Greensboro, NC: Center for Creative Leadership.

10. De Meuse, K. P., Dai, G., & Hallenbeck, G. S. (2010). Learning agility: A construct whose time has come. *Consulting Psychology Journal: Practice and Research, 62*(2).

11. Lombardo, M. M., & Eichinger, R. W. (2010). *Career Architect® development planner: A systematic approach to development including 103 research-based and experience-tested development plans and coaching tips* (5th ed.). Minneapolis, MN: Lominger International: A Korn/Ferry Company.

12. Eichinger, R. W., Lombardo, M. M., & Capretta, C. C. (2010). *FYI™ for learning agility.* Minneapolis, MN: Lominger International: A Korn/Ferry Company.

13. Sternberg, R. J., Wagner, R. K., Williams, W. M., & Horvath, J. A. (1995). Testing common sense. *American Psychologist, 50*(11), 912–927.

14. Swisher, V. V. (2012). *Becoming an agile leader: Know what to do when you don't know what to do.* Minneapolis, MN: Lominger International: A Korn/Ferry Company.

15. De Meuse, K., Dai, G., Eichinger, R., Page, R., Clark, L., & Zewdie, S. (2011). *The development and validation of a self assessment of learning agility* [Technical Report]. Los Angeles, CA: The Korn/Ferry Institute.

References

Self-Awareness: Seeking Personal Insight

Angelou, M. (1993). *The inaugural poem: On the pulse of morning.* New York, NY: Random House.

Angelou, M. (2004). *The collected autobiographies of Maya Angelou.* New York, NY: Random House.

Chacour, E. (with Hazard, D.). (2003). *Blood brothers: The unforgettable story of a Palestinian Christian working for peace in Israel* (Expanded ed.). Grand Rapids, MI: Chosen Books.

George, B. (with Sims, P.). (2007). *True north: Discover your authentic leadership.* San Francisco, CA: Jossey-Bass.

Maya Angelou. (n.d.). In *Wikipedia.* Retrieved January 29, 2012, from http://en.wikipedia.org/wiki/Maya_Angelou

Mental Agility: Making Fresh Connections

Finocchiaro, M. A. (2007, August 15). The person of the millennium: The unique impact of Galileo on world history, by M. Weidhorn [Book review]. *The Historian, 69*(3), 601–602. doi:10.1111/j.1540-6563.2007.00189_68.x

Galileo. (2001). *Dialogue concerning the two chief world systems.* (S. Drake, Trans.). New York, NY: Modern Library. (Original work published 1632.)

Isaacson, W. (2007). *Einstein: His life and universe.* New York, NY: Simon & Schuster.

Isaacson, W. (2011). *Steve Jobs.* New York, NY: Simon & Schuster.

Sharratt, M. (1994). *Galileo: Decisive innovator.* New York, NY: Cambridge University Press.

People Agility: Bringing Out the Best in Others

Ahtisaari, M. (2010, March 5). *Striving for peace: A question of will.* Keynote address at the 22nd Annual Nobel Peace Prize Forum, Minneapolis, MN.

Carlin, J. (2008). *Playing the enemy: Nelson Mandela and the game that made a nation.* New York, NY: The Penguin Press.

Keller, B. (2008). *Tree shaker: The story of Nelson Mandela.* Boston, MA: Kingfisher, a Houghton Mifflin Company.

King, L. (2000, May 16). President Nelson Mandela one-on-one [Interview Transcript]. *Larry King Live.* CNN. Retrieved February 28, 2012, from http://transcripts.cnn.com/TRANSCRIPTS/0005/16/lkl.00.html

Maharaj, M., & Kathrada, A. (Eds.). (2006). *Mandela: The authorized portrait.* Auckland, New Zealand: PQ Blackwell Limited.

Mandela, N. (1995). *Long walk to freedom: The autobiography of Nelson Mandela.* New York, NY: Little, Brown & Company.

Tannen, D. (1988, June 8). The TV host. *Time Magazine, 151*(22). Retrieved September 17, 2010, from http://www.time.com/time/magazine/article/0,9171,988512,00.html

Zoglin, R. (1988, August 8). Oprah Winfrey: Lady with a calling. *Time Magazine.*

Change Agility: Promoting New Possibilities

Counts, A. (2008). *Small loans, big dreams: How Nobel Prize winner Muhammad Yunus and microfinance are changing the world.* Hoboken, NJ: John Wiley & Sons.

Gabler, N. (2007). *Walt Disney: The triumph of the American imagination.* New York, NY: Vintage Books.

Nightingale, F. (1974). *Notes on Nursing.* New York, NY: Kaplan Publishing. (Original work published 1860.)

Yunus, M. (2007). *Banker to the poor: Micro-lending and the battle against world poverty* (Rev. and Updated). New York, NY: Public Affairs.

Results Agility: Making Things Happen

Ash, M. K. (2008). *The Mary Kay way: Timeless principles from America's greatest woman entrepreneur* (Updated ed.). Hoboken, NJ: John Wiley & Sons.

Earhart, A. (1937). *Last flight.* New York, NY: Harcourt, Brace and Company.

Lovell, M. S. (2009). *The sound of wings: The life of Amelia Earhart* (Reprint ed.). New York, NY: St. Martin's Griffin.

Thomas Edison. (n.d.). In *Wikipedia.* Retrieved April 23, 2012, from http://en.wikipedia.org/wiki/Thomas_Edison

Underwood, J. (2003). *More than a pink Cadillac: Mary Kay Inc.'s 9 leadership keys to success.* New York, NY: McGraw-Hill.

Acknowledgments

I wish to express deep appreciation to my colleagues who have made this book possible.

Thanks to Bob Eichinger and Mike Lombardo for the rich legacy of research, experience, and wisdom upon which this book is built.

Thanks to George Hallenbeck, Ken De Meuse, Vicki Swisher, Erica Lutrick, Guangrong Dai, and King Yii (Lulu) Tang for being great thought partners in the creation of this book.

Thanks to Kim Ruyle, David Grant, Karen Dorece, Dana Landis, Sian Connell, Zoe Hruby, Karen Opp, and Joanne Lee for suggestions and insights provided on early drafts.

Thanks to the core team of Stacy Rider, Eric Ekstrand, Leah Winckler, Diane Hoffmann Kotila, Lesley Kurke, Doug Lodermeier, Phil Boehlke, Bonnie Parks, La Tasha Reed, and Yasmin Salcedo for their hard work and dedication.

Resources for Individuals

In addition to the tips, recommendations, and suggestions for further reading in the Learning Agility chapters, here are some additional tools that can help you on your journey to explore and potentially build your Learning Agility.

Becoming an Agile Leader: Know What to Do…When You Don't Know What to Do explores the five key characteristics, or factors, of Learning Agility. Spotlighting well-known leaders from business and the world stage, *Becoming an Agile Leader* is filled with more than 70 practical development tips you can start using today to increase your own agility and help ensure success in those new, challenging assignments. So you will know what to do…when you don't know what to do.

Becoming an Agile Leader App can help you achieve greater self-awareness through capturing on-the-spot insights and reflections. *Becoming an Agile Leader* App provides inspiring, thought-provoking quotes related to the Learning Agility factors which will help you easily reflect, document, and transfer learnings from your experiences.

FYI™ for Insight will help you understand 21 leadership characteristics for success and 5 characteristics that can derail your career. It will also make you aware of *why* you may be lacking skill or motivation in certain areas. This is critical because becoming self-aware can get you 50% of the way toward improving your performance.

Insight into strengths and weaknesses can help you get what you want from your career. The *FYI™ for Insight* Self-Awareness Assessment is a three-step process that takes just a few minutes. A personalized report gives you a self-awareness score and highlights your hidden strengths and blind spots.

More information on these resources can be found at http://www.lominger.com

Resources for Organizations

Research has clearly shown that Learning Agility is a primary component and key differentiator of potential for leadership roles. By understanding and leveraging Learning Agility in your organization, you can better distinguish between current performance and future potential and create a more targeted, differentiated development strategy for current and future leaders. The assessment and development tools here can help you integrate Learning Agility into your organization's strategic talent management initiatives.

Assessments

viaEDGE™ easily and efficiently gauges the Learning Agility of large numbers of individuals, with the ease of an online self-administered assessment. viaEDGE™ helps organizations assess internal talent for placement and development of high potentials and can aid in external candidate hiring. *Available in multiple languages.*

Choices Architect® has been used for years by organizations to identify, validate, and select those who are the most learning agile. Choices Architect® scores have been significantly related to independent measures or ratings of potential, consistent performance, and staying out of trouble. This well-validated assessment is available in multiple formats, including an online multi-rater survey. *Available in multiple languages.*

Learning From Experience™ (LFE) Interview Guide is a selection tool designed to assist employers with assessing learning agility in the interviewing process. The guide helps organizations build future bench strength through interviewing and selecting the most learning agile internal and external candidates.

Development Tools

Learning Agility can be developed. *FYI™ for Learning Agility* is designed for any motivated person seeking to develop skills that lead to increased Learning Agility. It includes 200+ improvement and workaround strategies that individuals can use today on or off the job.

Are all highly learning agile individuals the same? The *High Learning Agility Profiles* guide helps learning agile individuals identify which of the seven distinct profiles best fits them, learn the situations that favor their learning agility strengths, and determine opportunities for further developing their learning agility.

More information on these resources can be found at http://www.lominger.com